INSP SOCCER STORIES

FOR
YOUNG READERS

*Mastering the Mental Toughness and Winning Mindset Strategies
to Become an Amazing Soccer Player*

BY

Halsey Kingsley

Table of Contents

Introduction

Welcome to "Inspiring Soccer Stories for Young Readers: Mastering the Mental Toughness and Winning Mindset Strategies to Become an Amazing Soccer Player." If you're passionate about soccer and dream of becoming an exceptional player, you've just picked up a book that will guide you on your journey to greatness.

Soccer is more than just a game; it's a beautiful dance of skill, strategy, and teamwork. It's a sport that transcends borders, languages, and cultures, uniting people from all walks of life in the pursuit of a common goal: victory on the pitch. Whether you're already lacing up your cleats or just starting to explore the world of soccer, this book is your key to unlocking the secrets of success in the world's most beloved sport.

Our adventure begins by delving into the rich history of soccer. From its origins in ancient civilizations to the modern game we know today, we'll explore how soccer has evolved over centuries, captivating the hearts of millions along the way. Understanding the roots of the sport will give you a deeper appreciation for the game and its enduring appeal.

Next, we'll dive into the basics of how to play soccer. Whether you're a forward, midfielder, defender, or goalkeeper, you'll discover the unique roles and positions that make up a soccer team. We'll also explore the rules of the game and how to avoid common fouls that can lead to penalties.

One of the most critical steps on your soccer journey is discovering your ideal position. Are you a natural striker who loves scoring goals, a midfield maestro who controls the game's tempo, or a fearless defender who protects the goal like a fortress? This book will help you find your place on the field and understand the strengths and responsibilities of each position.

As we progress, you'll encounter inspiring stories of young soccer players who persevered to achieve greatness. You'll meet the last line of defense, the midfield maestro, the goal machine, and other young athletes who want to become soccer legends. Their journeys will show you that with dedication, hard work, and the right mindset, you can overcome obstacles and reach your soccer goals.

But our journey doesn't stop there. We'll also introduce you to some of the greatest soccer players the world has ever seen. From Diego Maradona's magical dribbling to Cristiano Ronaldo's incredible athleticism, you'll learn about the iconic players who have left an indelible mark on the sport. Their stories will inspire you to dream big and aim high.

As you read this book, you'll not only gain a deeper understanding of soccer but also develop the mental toughness and winning mindset that are essential for success on the field. Soccer is not just about physical skills; it's about determination, resilience, and a never-give-up attitude. You'll learn from the best and be prepared to face the challenges that lie ahead in your soccer journey.

So, young reader, are you ready to embark on this exhilarating adventure into the world of soccer? Turn the page, kick off your shoes, and let's dive into "Inspiring Soccer Stories for Young Readers." It's time to take your first step towards becoming an amazing soccer player!

Soccer History

Have you ever wondered why some folks call it "*football*" while others insist on "*soccer*"? It's like having two names for the same magical adventure. But fear not, we're diving into the wonderful world of words to uncover the secret behind this linguistic mystery.

Now, let's kick things off with a little history lesson. Soccer wasn't born in America. It all began in England, where they fondly called it "*football*." So, you might think that "*soccer*" is an American invention, but it's not! The word "*soccer*" actually hails from British slang. But here's the kicker - most Brits today prefer the good old "*football*" name. Meanwhile, across the pond in the United States, "*football*" means something entirely different.

In the early days, using either "*football*" or "soccer" in England was a breeze, and nobody minded which term you used. It was all in the name of fun! But as the years rolled by, something changed. By the 1980s, the word "*soccer*" started to fade away in the UK, and the game we all adore became widely known as "*football*."

Fast forward to the middle of the 20th century, and "soccer" had become firmly established in American lingo. But here's the twist in our tale: it's not just the USA! Several other countries, like Canada, Ireland, Australia, New Zealand, South Africa, and Japan, also use the term "*soccer*" because they have their unique versions of football, creating the need for different names.

Soccer is a relatively young sport in the grand tapestry of human history. Sports had been a part of our lives for centuries, with the legendary Olympic Games dating back over 2,000 years. However, the soccer we know today didn't come into existence until the 1800s.

Before the birth of modern soccer, people across the globe played various ball games. In the far-off lands of ancient China, there was a game known as "*kuju*," and in Japan, they had a version called "*kamari*," which was like a delightful blend of soccer and hacky sack. Far to the west, in the mighty Roman Empire, a game called "*harpustum*" was played, resembling a rough and tumble version of rugby.

Even as different cultures crafted their own versions of ball games, it was during the Middle Ages that "*folk football*" began to take shape. This was the precursor to the soccer we know today, and it soon became a beloved pastime in England and beyond. However, there was a catch - the rules were a bit like a wild adventure! Each village and town had its unique rules.

This wild diversity in rules made it tricky for university students to come together and play when they reached higher learning institutions. Imagine trying to play with friends who thought different rules applied! Not exactly the best way to enjoy the game. Clearly, soccer needed a set of rules that everyone could agree upon.

In the year 1863, something magical happened. Twelve soccer clubs from around London united to form the "Football Association." Together, they crafted a set of rules that were printed and shared far and wide. These new regulations declared that it was against the rules to touch the ball with your hands, except for the brave goalkeepers. This declaration was the moment soccer distinguished itself from rugby, once and for all. Now, anyone, anywhere could play the beautiful game with the same rules. All they needed were a rule book, a ball, a field, and some nets.

With the rules now crystal clear, the game of soccer spread like wildfire across England and then to every corner of the globe. It became the most popular sport on our planet, bringing joy and excitement to people everywhere.

So, my young friends, next time you find yourself on the soccer field, you can impress your companions with this incredible tale of how soccer came to be, and maybe, you'll inspire them to love the game as much as you do. Whether you call it "*soccer*" or "*football*," remember that you're talking about the same thrilling game that unites people all around the world.

How to Play Soccer?

Soccer is a really fun team sport played with 11 players on each side, and they use a round ball.

The most important rule in soccer is that you can't touch the ball with your hands or arms while you're playing. But there's one special player on each team called the goalkeeper, and they can use their hands when they're protecting their goal.

A soccer game is divided into two halves, each lasting 45 minutes. The goal of the game is to score more goals than the other team in these 90 minutes.

Before the game begins, there's a coin toss to decide which team gets to choose which goal to attack first.

Now, let's talk about the soccer field. It's usually a big rectangular field with goals at each end.

In the middle of the field, there's a center line that cuts it in half. Right in the middle, there's a center circle, which is 10 yards wide.

The field has lines that mark its boundaries. The long sides of the field have lines called touchlines or sidelines, and the ends of the field have lines called goal lines or end lines.

There are special areas on the field too:

1. Goal Area: This is a box that goes six yards out from the goal posts. Free kicks can be taken from here.

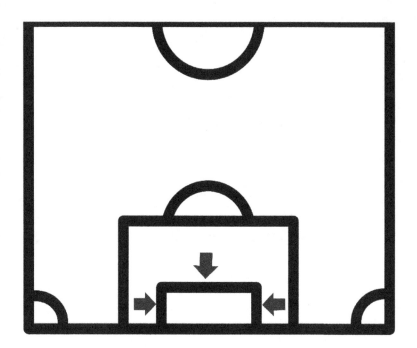

2. **Penalty Area:** It's a bigger box that extends 18 yards out from the goal posts. Goalkeepers can use their hands here, and if a defense player commits a foul here, the other team gets a penalty kick.

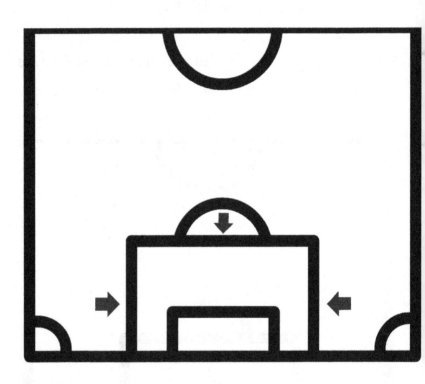

3. **Penalty Arc:** This is an arc at the top of the penalty box, and players, except the goalkeeper and the kicker, can't enter it during a penalty kick.

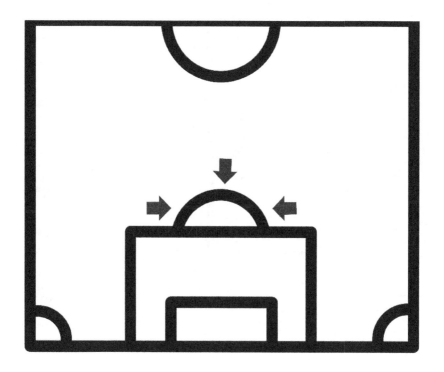

4. **Corners:** Each corner of the field has a flag post and a corner arc, which is one yard in diameter. When you take a corner kick, the ball has to be placed within this arc.

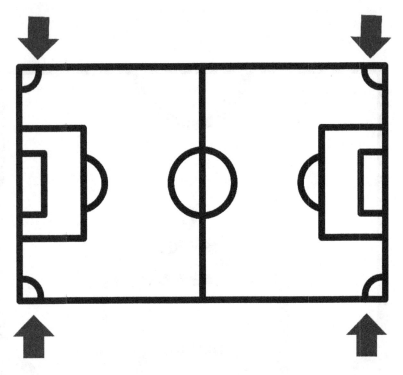

To score a goal, the whole ball needs to cross the line. If it does, you've got a point!

And finally, to win the game, you have to score more goals than the other team. It's as simple as that!

Roles and Positions

Have you ever wondered why soccer players wear numbers on their jerseys? Well, it's like having a secret code that helps us identify their positions on the field. But remember, the number on their shirt doesn't match the number on the field!

We'll focus on a typical 11-player game.

Number 1: The goalkeeper, also known as the "goalie," is the ultimate guardian of the goalpost. They're the only players allowed to use their hands to stop the ball, but only within their penalty area. Goalies wear special gloves and a different-colored jersey to stand out from the rest of the team. During penalty kicks, they transformed into the last line of defense, wielding their enchanted gloves to block shots and send the ball far away from harm's reach.

Number 2 and 3: Meet the right back and left back, like a dynamic duo working together on defense. They're a bit like twins, and they must communicate and coordinate throughout the game. When one of them joins the attack, the other holds back slightly to avoid leaving gaps in the defense.

Numbers 4 and 5: These are the center backs, the defenders in the heart of the team. Their main job is to protect the goal and stop the opponent from scoring.

Number 6: The defensive midfielder is like a secret agent in the midfield. They are responsible for stopping opponents, carrying the ball out of the danger zone, and passing it to their teammates. Think of them as the team's guardian in the middle of the field.

Number 8: The central midfielder is the heart of the team. They are like the conductors of an orchestra, distributing the ball, orchestrating the plays, and keeping the game flowing smoothly. It's a role that requires exceptional ball-handling and passing skills.

Number 10: The attacking midfielder, also known as the "playmaker," is a creative genius. They using their skills to score goals and create opportunities for their teammates. Think of them as the magic makers on the field.

Numbers 11 and 7: These are the left and right midfielders, also known as "wingers" or "outside midfielders." They stay wide on the field and help stretch the opponent's defense, creating space for their offensive teammates. These players need strong one-on-one skills to get past the opponent's fullbacks.

Number 9: The center forward or striker is the one many of you have been waiting for. Their main job is to score goals in whatever way possible. Whether it's dribbling past defenders or positioning themselves perfectly to receive passes, they are the ultimate goal-getters.

The most common formation known as the 4-4-2. This magical formation consisted of four defenders, four midfielders, and two forwards. Each position had a specific area of the field to guard, much like knights protecting their castle.

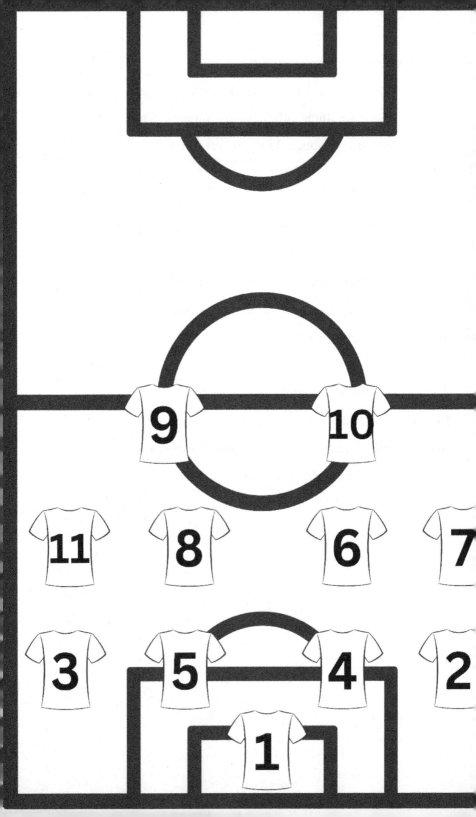

Discovering Your Ideal Position

"What position do you play?" Some of you may already have a clear-cut answer, proudly proclaiming yourselves as midfielders, wingers, or fullbacks. But what if you're still unsure about where you belong on the pitch?

Selecting the perfect soccer position is akin to embarking on a heroic quest to find your destiny in the beautiful game. There are a few approaches to finding the right fit, but one of the simplest is to consider what you genuinely enjoy doing on the soccer field and which position excites you the most.

If you relish being at the heart of the action, orchestrating the game's flow, and savor having the ball at your feet, then the role of a central midfielder might be your calling. Here, you'll be at the epicenter of every play, pulling the strings.

For those of you who thrive on physicality, tackling, and relish duels, defensive positions beckon. You'll become the guardians of your team's goal, ensuring that the opposition finds it nearly impossible to breach your defenses.

Is dribbling past opponents, having the ball at your feet, and creating goal-scoring opportunities your idea of soccer bliss? If so, taking up the mantle of a winger could be your path to glory.

Do you dream of being the hero who scores the decisive goals, possess the speed to leave defenders in your wake, and boast a killer instinct in front of the net? Then the striker's role might be your true calling.

Perhaps you enjoy both defending and supporting attacks, possess agility, and are quick on your feet. In that case, full back or wing back positions could be your realm, covering extensive ground both defensively and offensively.

If you're strong, composed under pressure, and excel at positioning, you might thrive as a center back. Here, you'll be the unyielding fortress in front of your goalkeeper, thwarting every attempt to breach your defenses.

For those gifted with precise passing, dribbling skills, vision, and creativity, the role of an attacking midfielder awaits.

You'll be the artist on the canvas, crafting opportunities for your team.

If you combine strength, tackling prowess, and an innate sense of controlling the game, then the central defensive midfielder position is your stage. Your mission: disrupt the opponent's play and distribute the ball.

Are you brave, unafraid of the ball, and blessed with lightning-fast reflexes? You might have what it takes to be the guardian of the net, the last line of defense.

But here's the secret ingredient: Adaptability. Your coach might spot potential in you that you haven't recognized. They could recommend a different position that harnesses your skills and benefits the team. Don't shy away from trying it out; you might unearth a hidden talent.

If you love making big saves and being the hero, being a goalkeeper might be the perfect position for you! Goalkeepers need to be super quick, brave, and have amazing reflexes because they need to jump, dive, and use their hands and feet to keep the ball out of the net. They're like the last line of defense, and their job is crucial to keeping the other team from scoring.

Remember, soccer is about enjoyment and pursuing your dreams. If you're passionate about a specific position, chase it with all your heart! Continuously hone your skills, and who knows, you might become the next soccer legend. So, what's your soccer destiny?

Soccer Rules

Soccer rules are easy to understand! Here's how it works:

1. **No Hands, Except for Goalies:** You can't touch the ball with your hands or arms, unless you're the goalie. They can use their hands in their goal area.

2. **Goal = Ball Completely Crosses the Line:** To score a goal, the whole ball must go over the line. It's like when you score in a game. You know you've done it right when you see the ball completely inside the goal.

3. **Referees:** There's a special person called a referee who makes sure everyone plays by the rules. They have two friends called assistant referees to help them.

4. **Game Time:** A game is split into two halves, each lasting 45 minutes. There's a 15-minute break in between. If teams are tied after 90 minutes, they might play extra time, which is 30 more minutes in two halves. If it's still tied, they use a penalty shootout to pick the winner.

5. **Kickoff:** At the start of each half and after a goal, there's a kickoff from the center circle. All players must stay on their side of the field, except for the one doing the kickoff.

6. **Player Substitutions:** Teams can have up to seven substitute players. They can switch players at any time during the game, but only three times per half. If a player gets hurt and they've already made three subs, tough luck, they have to play short-handed.

7. **Offside Rule:** This rule helps keep things fair. You can't hang out near the opponent's goal waiting for the ball. You need to be behind the last defender when the ball is passed to you. If not, it's a free-kick for the other team.

8. **Throw-In:** When the ball goes out of bounds, the other team gets to throw it in from where it went out. You have to throw it from behind your head, using both hands, and keep both feet on the ground.

9. **Corner Kick:** If the defending team touches the ball last before it goes out of bounds near their goal, the other team gets to kick it from the corner.

10. **Goal Kick:** When the offensive team touches the ball last before it goes out of bounds behind the goal, the goalie gets to kick it from their goal box.

11. **Penalty Kick:** If there's a foul in the penalty area, the fouled team gets a special free kick called a penalty kick.

12. **Free Kicks:** Sometimes, the referee gives a free kick or penalty kick for a foul. It's a chance for the other team to make a play.

13. **Out of Bounds:** When the ball goes completely out of bounds, the other team gets it from where it went out.

14. **Fouls:** If a player does something not allowed, like tripping, pushing, or using their hands, the ref can give them a yellow card (a warning) or a red card (kicked out of the game). If you get two yellow cards, it's like getting a red card.

Now you know the basic rules of soccer. It's all about running, kicking, and having fun with your team!

Soccer Fouls

There are two types of fouls: direct kick fouls and indirect kick fouls. Let's break it down!

Direct Kick Fouls

These are the big ones. When one team commits a foul, the other team gets a direct free kick. Here are the main direct kick fouls:

1. **Kicking Too Hard**: If a player kicks or tries to kick an opponent super hard on purpose, it's a foul.

2. **Tripping with Force:** Tripping someone recklessly and with force is a no-no.

3. **Charging Like a Bull:** Charging recklessly into an opponent or using excessive force is a foul.

4. **Striking Out:** If a player strikes or tries to strike an opponent way too hard, that's not cool.

5. **Pushing Power:** Pushing another player, even the goalkeeper, with too much force is against the rules.

6. **Jumping into Trouble:** Jumping at an opponent, even with your head, in a reckless way is a foul.

7. **No Grabbing:** Grabbing or pulling an opponent's jersey or clothes in an obvious way is a foul.

8. **Early Contact:** Touching an opponent before touching the ball during a tackle is a foul.

9. **Spit It Out:** Spitting at an opponent, whether it hits them or not, is not okay.

10. **Hand Play:** Deliberately using your hands to handle the ball is a foul. Remember, no hands allowed except for the goalie!

Indirect Kick Fouls

These fouls result in an indirect free kick for the other team. There are two categories: one for all players and one just for goalies.

For All Players:

1. **Dangerous Play:** If a player is being reckless and might hurt someone, it's a foul.

2. **Blocking the Way:** Using your body to block an opponent's movements, even accidentally, is a foul.

3. **Keeper Troubles:** Preventing the goalkeeper from releasing the ball from their hands by standing in their way is a foul.

For Goalies Only

1. **Time Limit:** A goalkeeper can't hold the ball for more than six seconds.

2. **No Hands After a Kick:** If a teammate deliberately kicks the ball to the goalie, they can't use their hands.

3. **Throw-In Trouble:** If a goalie receives a throw-in from a teammate and then touches the ball with their hands, it's a foul.

4. **Quick Hands:** After releasing the ball, a goalie can't touch it again with their hands before another player does.

And that's the scoop on soccer fouls! Remember these rules, play fair, and have a blast on the field.

STORIES OF YOUNG SOCCER PLAYERS

Hey, I'm Noah, and I'm the goalkeeper for my soccer team. Let me take you on a journey into my world as a goalie, where I get to be the hero on the field!

Being a goalkeeper is like having a super cool superpower. It all starts with the gear. I get to wear this awesome goalie jersey and these special gloves that make me feel invincible. They're like my armor, helping me face anything that comes my way. And believe me, I need all the gear because I'm the last line of defense.

My main mission is to stop the other team from scoring goals. That's my number one job. It's not just about diving to make amazing saves, although that's a big part of it. It's about being a hero for my team.

When the other team tries to kick the ball into our goal, I'm there to block it. I use my hands to make fingertip saves, just like a superhero catching a speeding bullet. I dive left, I dive right, I dive forward, and I even leap high into the air to stop the ball from going into the net. It's like I can fly for a split second, and it's the best feeling in the world.

But being a goalie is about more than just stopping shots. I have to be really good with my feet too. Sometimes, I have to kick the ball really far down the field to start an attack for my team. It's like being a quarterback in American football, but with soccer! I have to make sure my kicks are accurate and powerful, just like a superhero's laser beam.

What's even more amazing is that I have to be super aware of everything happening on the field. I scan the entire pitch to see where the other team's players are and where my teammates are. That way, I can shout out instructions to my team and help them make the right moves. I get to be the eyes and voice on the field, guiding my team to victory.

But here's the best part: I get to be the team's guardian angel. I'm always on the lookout for the ball, making sure it doesn't sneak into our goal. I have to be quick, agile, and ready to pounce at any moment. It's a big responsibility, but it's also a lot of fun.

So, being a goalie is like being a superhero for my soccer team. I stop shots, make amazing saves, help my teammates by being the eyes and voice on the field, and even kick the ball like a pro. And you know what the best part is? I absolutely love being in goal and saving the day for my team! It's not just a position; it's a thrilling adventure every time I step onto the field.

THE MIDFIELD MAESTRO

Hey there, young readers! My name is Jackson, and I play as an attacking midfielder on my soccer team. I'm excited to share more about my role on the field and what makes it so much fun. So, grab your soccer gear, and let's dive into the exciting world of being an attacking midfielder!

To begin, being an attacking midfielder is like being the team's playmaker. I get to help my team score goals, and that's the best part of the game! Imagine I'm wearing a red jersey, and we're trying to score goals against the blue team. Here's a closer look at my role.

One of the coolest things about my position is the freedom to move all around the field. I'm not tied to one spot like some other players. This makes it really tricky for the other team because they can't guess where I'll be next. It's like playing a game of hide and seek on the soccer field!

As an attacking midfielder, I get to decide when to come close to my teammates for short passes or sprint into open spaces to receive long passes. It's like having a secret code with my teammates - we pass the ball to each other to outsmart the other team. Sometimes, it's a quick game of catch, and other times, it's like passing a message in a bottle across a big ocean.

My main job is to hang out in places where I can help my team attack and, of course, score goals. I don't like to stay too far back; I want to be close to the opponent's goal. That's where all the action happens! It's like being at the front row of a magic show, where all the magic happens up close.

To keep the other team guessing, I change up my runs. I make sudden, surprise runs into open spaces. This confuses the defenders and makes it really hard for them to keep an eye on me. It's a bit like playing a game of tag, where you have to be quick and tricky!

One of the most important things I've learned is to predict where the ball will be, not just where it is right now. It's a bit like guessing where your friend will throw a water balloon before they even throw it. Being there at the right time is super important! So, I always try to think a few steps ahead.

Soccer is all about teamwork. I pass the ball to my teammates, make runs to create space, and get the ball back. Teamwork is like having a secret code with your friends to solve a puzzle together. It's like being part of an awesome club where everyone has their role.

When my team is trying to score, I rush into the opponent's penalty area. It's like trying to get to the front of the line when your favorite ice cream truck arrives. I want to be there in case the ball comes my way, ready to score a fantastic goal!

I never stop moving on the field. I show for the ball, make runs, and keep on running. Moving is like dancing on the field, and it helps me stay involved in the game. It's like being in a non-stop dance party with my teammates!

Being an attacking midfielder is like being the captain of a ship, steering it towards victory. So, if you ever play as an attacking midfielder like me, have a blast, be creative, and help your team score lots of goals! Remember, soccer is all about smiles, high-fives, and celebrating with your teammates. So, go out there and have a fantastic time on the soccer field!

Hey, I'm Sammy, and I'm here to share more about my role as a soccer forward. I'm not just any forward; I'm the team's goal-scoring machine! But being a forward means I do more than just put the ball in the net. Let me take you through all the exciting things I do on the field.

First and foremost, my primary job is to score goals. I'm like the team's secret weapon when it comes to putting the ball in the back of the net. But guess what? I can also help out in other ways, making me super valuable to my team.

One of the coolest things I do is defend from the front. It's like playing offense and defense all at once. Imagine playing tag with the opponents – I love it! I chase down players and make them nervous. Sometimes, they even make mistakes, and that's when we get the ball back. It's like I'm a superhero, swooping in to save the day!

But wait, I don't just run around aimlessly. I pick my moments carefully. If I'm close to an opponent, and I know I can steal the ball, I go for it. I'm quick, and I can surprise them. But if I'm the only one pressing, I'm smart about it because I want to save my energy for when we're attacking. It's like conserving my superpowers for the right moment.

Now, when I don't have the ball, I'm not just standing around waiting for something to happen. That's not my style. I'm always on the move, making it easier for my teammates to pass the ball to me. Sometimes, I show both of my feet, asking for the ball. Other times, I sneak behind defenders to surprise them. I'm like a ninja on the field, creating space for myself to receive passes.

Timing is everything, though. I keep a close eye on the last defender, so I don't accidentally go offside. I start my runs early so I can get the ball just as I pass that defender. It's like a race against time, and I love every second of it!

When I find myself in the box, close to the opponent's goal, that's when the real fun begins. I make smart runs to get open for passes. Sometimes I sprint across the defender to the front post, hoping to tap the ball into the net. Other times, I peel off to the back post, waiting for a high pass to come my way. And if my teammates are drawing defenders away, I hang around at the top of the box, ready for a perfect pass.

But hold on, when I have the ball, I'm super careful. I don't just charge into a crowd of defenders or shoot when it's too crowded. I make sure to pass to open teammates or take a shot when I see a great chance. It's all about making the right decision at the right time. I want to score goals, but I also want my team to succeed.

However, don't get me wrong; I absolutely love scoring goals. I'm a bit greedy when it comes to that – in a good way! If I see an opportunity to shoot and score, you bet I'll take it. And when the ball hits the back of the net, it's like a celebration party on the field!

So, that's my role as a soccer forward. I score goals, defend from the front, make clever moves without the ball, and take care of it when I have it. It's a lot of hard work, but it's also incredibly fun, and I wouldn't trade it for anything in the world!

IN THE SHADOW
OF
THE SIDELINE

Hey there, young soccer enthusiasts! My name is Noah, and I'm here to introduce you to the thrilling world of being a winger in soccer. Grab your imaginary soccer boots, and let's embark on an exciting journey where I'll explain my role in detail.

First things first, my role as a winger is all about being unpredictable, just like a skilled magician. I don't want the defenders to know my every move. Sometimes, I stay wide on the wing, as wide as a superhero's cape fluttering in the wind. This helps create lots of space not just for me but also for my teammates. Imagine it's like a wide-open highway for us to work our magic on. But guess what? I don't stop there!

I also like to change things up by coming inside towards the middle of the field. It's like I'm sneaking into a secret treasure cave. When I do this, I can ask for the ball, pass it to my teammates, or even take an exciting shot on goal. And if I'm feeling extra adventurous, I might make a lightning-fast run behind the defenders, just like a superhero making a daring escape. It's all about keeping my opponents on their toes!

Imagine I have super-speed boots on. When I get the ball, I don't hesitate for a second. Nope, not me! Being direct is my superpower. I'm like a superhero zooming in to save the day. I take a quick touch and move forward with confidence. Hesitating would be like letting the bad guys catch up, and we definitely don't want that!

If you're running towards your favorite ice cream truck and you see your favorite flavor, you don't stop and think, you just go for it! That's how I approach the game – quick and decisive, like a superhero making split-second decisions to protect the city.

Now, here's a secret weapon I have - getting to the back post. Whenever one of my teammates is about to kick the ball into the box, I make a run to the back post. This is where I can score easy goals, just like a superhero scoring an easy win. It's all about positioning and being in the right place at the right time. Just like how superheroes are always ready to save the day!

But being a winger isn't just about scoring goals, it's also about stopping the other team. I don't leave my fullback teammate to defend all alone. That would be like leaving the gates of my castle unguarded! Instead, I rush back to help out when the opponents are attacking. It's like being a knight protecting my castle!

When the other team has the ball, I put pressure on their defenders. I'm like a superhero trying to stop the villains from getting away. If I do it right, they might make mistakes, and my team can win the ball back. It's all about teamwork, and I'm there to support my teammates just like superheroes have each other's backs!

So there you have it, my friends! Being a winger is like being a superhero on the soccer field. I get to be unpredictable, direct, score cool tap-in goals, and help my team defend. Remember these tips, and you'll be a soccer superstar in no time! Keep having fun and playing the beautiful game, and who knows, maybe you'll become a superhero on the soccer field too!

THE FORTIFIED WALL

Hi, all young future soccer stars! My name is Danny, and I want to tell you about my favorite role on the soccer field - being a defender! It's a cool position, and I'm excited to share some tips with you.

So, let's dive right in with the first question: "Where should I be?" When you're a defender, you're like a guardian of your team's goal. Picture it like you're the goalie's trusty sidekick. When our team loses the ball, I don't waste a second. I sprint back to my position on the field. It's like solving a puzzle, and I want to fit perfectly into our team's formation, just like it's drawn on the coach's plan.

Now, let's tackle the second question: "What should I do?" When I'm the closest player to the ball, it's like I'm the first line of defense. I don't let the other team get comfy. I run up to the player with the ball and try to make their life tough. Think of it like a game of tag, but I want to win every time. I force them to make mistakes or pass where I want them to, not where they want to.

But here's where it gets really exciting. If I'm not the closest to the ball, I become a bit like a secret agent. I think ahead and try to guess where the ball will go next. I want to be there before it arrives. So I get close to the player I'm marking, but I also stay inside and goal side. It's like I'm guarding our goal and their player at the same time.

Now, there are two important things I never forget: fitness and focus. To be a great defender, I need to be super fit. It's like having endless energy to run around and stay where I should be. And I must stay focused all the time. Even when I'm tired, I keep asking myself those two questions: "Where should I be?" and "What should I do?"

Being a defender is amazing because it's like being the goalie's bodyguard. I hope you remember these tips and have loads of fun defending on the soccer field. Share this with your friends and teammates, and remember to stay fit and focused. You'll be a fantastic defender just like me!

THE FULLBACK CHRONICLES

Hey there, young soccer fans! I'm Aiden, and I'm a fullback on our awesome soccer team. Today, I'm going to tell you all about my role on the field and how I make magic happen!

So, picture this: I'm the guy who guards the sides of the field. You can call me the "Wide Warrior." I'm like a superhero with my incredible speed and teamwork skills. But being a fullback isn't just about defending; it's also about attacking, and that's the best part!

I've got one special buddy on the field – my winger. We're like Batman and Robin, always working together to save the day. When I get the ball, I have a cool move called the "overlapping run." That means I pass the ball to my winger and sprint past them to create more space. It's like a secret code between us.

Now, here's the magic part: I want to put the ball in the perfect spot for my teammates to score. Sometimes, I send in a "cross" into the box, like a gift just waiting to be unwrapped. It's like making a wish, and my teammates are the ones who get to make it come true.

But wait, what if my winger is on the other side of the field? No problem! I still help them out by getting closer to them. It's like having their back. If things get tricky, I'm there to save the day.

And here's a super cool trick: I can quickly pass the ball to my teammates and then zoom forward like a rocket. I'm always super wide on the field because that's my secret weapon. It stretches the field like elastic, making it harder for the other team to stop us.

Now, here's the thing about defending. When the ball is on the opposite side of the field, I slide closer to my center-back buddies. We become a defensive shield, ready to protect our goal. But if the ball suddenly switches to my side, I'm like a lightning bolt – I grab it and start our attack. No free passes for the other team!

When it's time to deliver those fantastic crosses, I remember the golden rule: quality over quantity. I aim for the "second six," that magical spot between the penalty spot and the six-yard box. That's where the action happens. I can go for the byline and whip it across or send an early cross before the defense can blink.

And guess what? I don't always have to beat a defender to put in a fantastic cross. Sometimes, all it takes is a well-placed ball into space where my teammates can attack it.

So, that's my life as a fullback – part defender, part attacker, and all-around soccer superhero. I stay fit, work with my winger, spread wide like a boss, and defend like a champ. It's a thrilling adventure on the soccer field, and I wouldn't trade it for anything. Keep practicing, young soccer stars, and one day you might become an amazing fullback just like me!

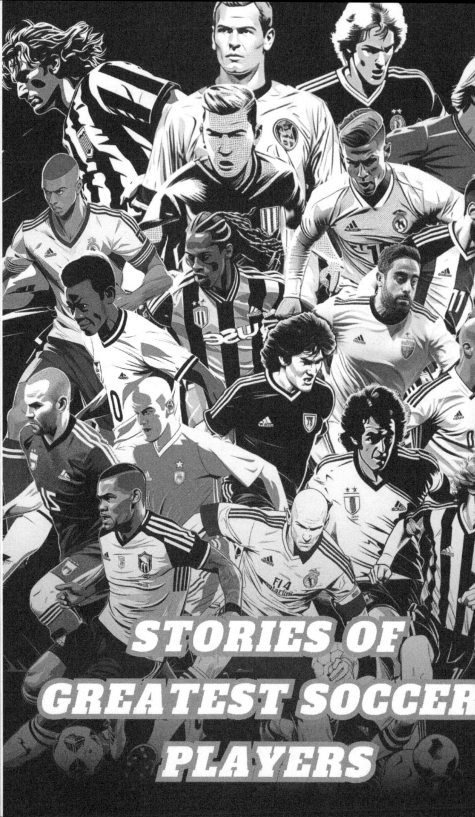

STORIES OF GREATEST SOCCER PLAYERS

Once upon a time, in the year 1960, there lived a young boy named Diego Armando Maradona in a place called Villa Fiorito. It was a tough neighborhood on the outskirts of Buenos Aires, filled with crumbling houses, garbage strewn about, and the constant presence of drugs and violence. Diego's family didn't have much. His dad, Diego Senior, worked hard in a factory to put food on the table for their seven kids. His mom, Dona Tota, did her best to take care of the family and educate the children.

But life was a struggle. Dona Tota would often complain of stomach-aches, which prevented her from eating. In reality, it was because there wasn't enough food to go around. The family made many sacrifices to make ends meet.

One of the most significant sacrifices was buying a soccer ball for Diego's third birthday. It wasn't just any ball; it was a symbol of hope. With that ball, Diego displayed his incredible skills week after week, putting on a show for the people of Fiorito. He knew that this ball could change his family's future, and he was determined to succeed.

Diego joined his first soccer club, Argentinos Juniors, at the age of eight. Despite being shorter than most kids his age, Diego was muscular and had unmatched skills. Some people even accused him of being older and suffering from dwarfism. His mother had to produce his birth certificate to prove he was just eight.

Now, with the right to play, Diego's presence on the field was immense. Defenders couldn't take the ball from him. His technique and leg strength allowed him to beat any opponent. He quickly became a target for the opposition's parents, who didn't understand how this kid, so different and from a poor background, could be better than their children. But Diego responded on the pitch, where he had one goal – scoring.

His first coach, Francisco Cornejo, believed that the hatred directed at Diego only made him better. It fueled his competitive spirit, which was evident even at the age of 12 when he played for a soda. He was as competitive then as he would be at 25 in the World Cup.

Argentinos Juniors wanted to help Diego become even stronger. So, when he turned 15, they provided him with an apartment near the stadium to make training easier. His first paycheck went toward buying his parents a television.

Diego knew that to achieve his dreams, he had to move into the professional ranks. Just ten days before his 16th birthday, he became the youngest player in history to play in the Argentine first division. The crowds chanted his name as soon as he stepped onto the pitch. Diego's success was fueled by the hatred aimed at him. It energized and motivated him.

Imagine, a teenager stepping onto the big stage. And he didn't just play; he scored his first goal only two weeks after turning 16. In five seasons, he scored a whopping 116 goals in 166 appearances.

Maradona's time at Barcelona was impressive. In his first season, he scored 23 goals in 35 matches and helped win the Copa del Rey. And guess what? He was the first of only three players ever to be applauded by Real Madrid fans during an El Clasico match!

In the 1986 World Cup held in Mexico, he was unstoppable. He single-handedly carried Argentina to victory, winning the tournament and being named the best player. Maradona played every minute, scored five goals, and provided five assists.

He wanted to represent the excluded population from his neighborhood, and he played with the intention of saving his family from poverty. Diego Maradona was always fueled by his past, his betrayals, his fragile health, and his addiction. He carried these injuries throughout his life but never stopped playing.

Diego Maradona's love for soccer and his unwavering spirit, much like an inner child, drove him to become one of the greatest players in history. His legacy remains, and he will forever be remembered for his indomitable spirit on the soccer field.

XAVI
HERNÁNDEZ

In the year 1999, there was an 18-year-old kid with a dream. He was plucked from FC Barcelona's youth program, La Masia, and placed right into the starting lineup of the men's team. You might wonder why this is such a big deal. Well, he wasn't just any ordinary kid. His name was Xavi Hernandez, and he was about to embark on a journey that would change the world of soccer forever.

Imagine a young, seemingly small, slow, and not very strong kid was asked to step in and replace the team's injured captain. It sounded crazy to many fans and even some players. After all, to outsiders, this kid appeared too small and too weak to face grown men on the soccer field. But Xavi was about to prove them all wrong.

In that year, Xavi helped Barcelona secure the league title, and it was just the beginning. Over the next decade, he would become one of the greatest midfielders in the history of soccer, known for his incredible vision and playmaking abilities.

Xavi's journey started in a small town where soccer was a way of life. His father ran a local youth club, and from a very young age, Xavi was surrounded by the beautiful game. At just 11 years old, Barcelona scouts spotted his talent and invited him to join their prestigious youth program, La Masia. It was a place where future soccer legends were born.

One day, Xavi's youth coach asked Pep Guardiola, who was a star player for Barcelona's men's team at the time, to watch Xavi during training. Guardiola was amazed by what he saw. He joked that Xavi might take his place in the first team someday. Little did they know that this joke would turn into reality.

In 1998, at the age of 18, Xavi made his senior team debut for Barcelona, scoring the only goal in a match against Mallorca. Barcelona was struggling in the league before that match, but Xavi's arrival changed everything. They went on to win the league title, and Xavi became a national sensation, earning the title of La Liga Breakthrough Player of the Year.

Xavi was small and not very fast, but he had an incredible football IQ. His passing and playmaking abilities were out of this world. Even his teammates, including legends like Rivaldo and Luis Figo, were in awe of him. Rivaldo said that Xavi kept things simple, moving at a calm pace on the field but always making the right play.

Xavi's influence on Barcelona continued to grow. In 2000, he helped Spain win silver in the Olympics, a sign of things to come. In 2004, under the guidance of manager Frank Rijkaard, Barcelona found its style of play, and Xavi became a co-captain at the age of 23.

The 2005-2006 season marked the pinnacle of Xavi's career at Barcelona. The team won the Champions League, La Liga, and the Spanish Super Cup. Xavi was the heart of the offense. Xavi's ability to control the tempo of the game was legendary.

But it wasn't just at the club level where Xavi shone. In the 2008 European Championship, Spain, led by Xavi, Iniesta, and David Silva, showcased a new style of play that focused on possession and technique.

Xavi's influence on Barcelona and Spain was immeasurable. In 2010, he helped Spain win its first World Cup title, and he continued to excel at the club level, winning more titles with

Barcelona. His accolades piled up, including multiple Ballon d'Or nominations.

When Xavi left Barcelona, the team struggled, highlighting his importance. However, in 2021, Xavi returned to the club as a coach. Under his guidance, Barcelona began to regain its form, signing new talent and nurturing young players.

Xavi's journey from a small town to soccer stardom was a testament to his incredible skill, vision, and intelligence on the field. He wasn't just a player; he was a maestro who changed the way the game was played. His impact on Barcelona, Spain, and the world of soccer will be remembered for generations to come.

ANDRÉS
INIESTA

In the land of Spain, May 1984, a talented boy named Andres Iniesta came into the world. He was born in the cozy town of Albacete, and from the very beginning, it seemed like he had a touch of magic in his feet.

Andres was a happy kid, and he had everything a young boy could wish for. But he also had something unique – a deep love for soccer. From the moment he could kick a ball, he was in love with the beautiful game. He played for his local club, Albacete, when he was just ten years old, and he played like a true gentleman on the field.

Imagine a young Andres, a tiny dynamo, dribbling past opponents as if they were ghosts and dancing on the soccer field to delight the fans. It wasn't just a game for him; it was his calling. His talent didn't go unnoticed, and soon, a big club came calling.

That club was none other than the mighty FC Barcelona. They saw something special in Andres Iniesta. So, off he went to Barcelona, leaving behind his parents and his cozy hometown. It was a tough goodbye, and he cried many tears. Young

Andres was a shy boy who kept to himself, but his passion for soccer burned brightly.

At the tender age of 15, he was already a captain and a leader on the field. At 17, he led Spain to victory in the UEFA European Under-17 Championship. But there was another player who shared his destiny, Xavi. Xavi was a senior player, and he had heard about a young talent at La Masia who was setting the pitch on fire. The first time he saw Iniesta play was during the 1999 Nike Cup.

It was clear to him that he was witnessing the rise of a future star who would eventually replace him. Even back then, his talent was so evident that the great Pep Guardiola, after watching Iniesta play, famously told Xavi, "You are going to retire me, but this kid will retire us all."

Xavi and Iniesta's first moments on the pitch together were magical. They seemed to have a telepathic connection, passing the ball back and forth effortlessly. They made it look like a friendly kickabout, even against strong opponents.

While Lionel Messi often received the spotlight for Barcelona's success, Xavi and Iniesta were the unsung heroes. They orchestrated the midfield, spraying passes, and making everything look easy. Under the guidance of coach Pep Guardiola, their style of possession football became the norm at Barcelona. They were the artists of free-flowing football. They became the heart of Barcelona's midfield.

Andres Iniesta showed the world what he was made of. The seasons of 2004 and 2005 were his breakout years, playing in an astonishing 37 out of 38 league games – more than any other player. Barcelona won La Liga, and Iniesta played a crucial role in their success.

But it was in the 2005-2006 season that Iniesta truly began to shine. He even played in the Champions League final. However, after that season, he was moved around by different coaches as they searched for his best position. Iniesta excelled wherever he played, but his heart belonged to the midfield.

In 2008, he had the honor of wearing the legendary number eight shirt, and from then on, magic flowed from his boots. Barcelona became the best club in the world, winning everything in sight – six out of six titles, a feat only two teams have ever achieved. Iniesta played a pivotal role in their victories, contributing with crucial goals and assists.

One unforgettable moment was his goal against Chelsea, which secured Barcelona's place in the Champions League final. They went on to defeat Manchester United in a dominant display. Even the legendary Sir Alex Ferguson couldn't help but praise Iniesta, calling him "fantastic" and emphasizing his importance to Barcelona.

But Iniesta's greatness extended beyond his footballing skills. He was known for his sportsmanship and elegance on the field. In fact, he is one of the few players who never received a red card. Fans lovingly nicknamed him "Don Andre" in recognition of his gentlemanly conduct.

In 2010, something extraordinary happened. Spain won the World Cup, and guess who scored the winning goal in the final? It was none other than Andres Iniesta himself. Yet, despite his remarkable achievements, he remained a bit underappreciated, a hidden gem in the world of soccer.

As the years went by, Iniesta continued to weave his magic on the pitch. He was instrumental in Barcelona's 2011-2012 season and, once again, finished third in the Ballon d'Or rankings. His legend grew with each passing season, and he helped Barcelona secure more titles, including the Champions League in 2015.

When you look at the statistics, they tell an impressive story: 89 goals and 162 assists in 861 games. But Iniesta's true brilliance couldn't be captured by numbers alone. His elegance, precision, and sheer love for the game were something you had to witness firsthand.

In the world of soccer, Andres Iniesta is celebrated as one of the greatest midfielders in history. His collection of honors and individual titles is proof of his exceptional talent. But more than that, he left an indelible mark on the hearts of fans worldwide.

So, the next time you watch a soccer match, keep an eye out for that touch of magic on the field. It might just remind you of Andres Iniesta, the true magician of soccer.

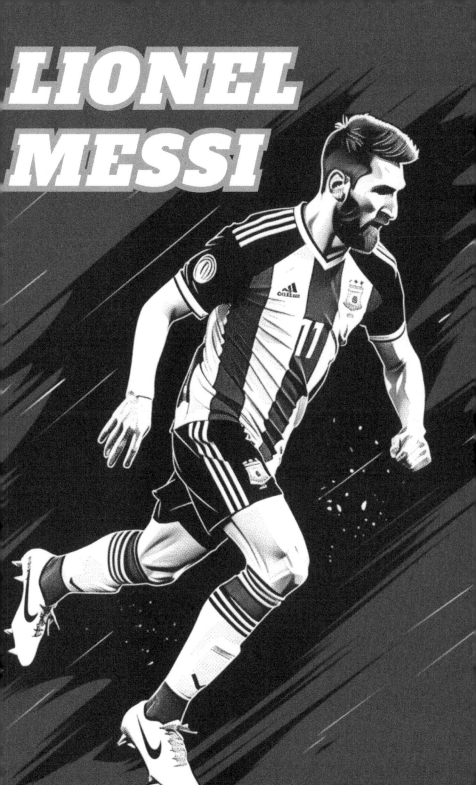

LIONEL
MESSI

Lionel Messi was a wizard with a soccer ball, and his skills were beyond imagination. He was born on a warm summer day in 1987 to a family that loved soccer more than anything else in the world. His father worked in a steel factory, and his mother cleaned houses part-time. The Messis were not a rich family, but they were hardworking and humble, and they instilled those values in their young son, Messi.

Messi just a kid from Argentina. He possessed a talent so extraordinary that it took him from being an ordinary boy to an unbelievable wonderkid. His journey led him from the streets of Argentina to the grand arenas of Barcelona, and along the way, soccer saved his life.

From a very early age, it was clear that Messi had a special talent for soccer. He was only five when he began playing for a local club, and guess who his coach was? His very own dad! As the years passed, his passion for soccer grew stronger.

When he was just eight years old, he joined a youth team called Newell's Old Boys. But there was a problem – Messi was much shorter than the other boys his age. He was diagnosed with something called "growth hormone deficiency." That meant he couldn't grow like other kids his age, and he needed special treatments that cost $900 every month. These injections were expensive, and his family couldn't afford them.

But then, something incredible happened. A famous soccer club called Barcelona heard about Messi's talent and his struggles. The coach offered him a trial, which meant Messi would get to prove himself, and if he succeeded, the club would cover his medical bills. So, they packed their bags and moved to Spain, where 12-year-old Messi became part of Barcelona's famous La Masia Academy.

At first, Messi felt homesick being so far away from his family and his beloved Argentina. But soon, he started to shine as part of Barcelona's legendary Baby Dream Team. People from all over Spain marveled at this young boy who had come from so far away to follow his dreams.

As the years went by, Messi's talent continued to amaze everyone. He scored goal after goal in the youth teams, and it wasn't long before he made his debut in the first team. At just 17 years old, he became the youngest player to ever represent Barcelona in La Liga. And when he scored his first goal against Albacete in 2005, he became Barcelona's youngest goal scorer.

As he grew and played more, Messi's skills became legendary. He demonstrated his magic with each game. He faced challenges and injuries but never stopped playing. Messi's determination and love for the game set him apart.

One of the most magical moments of Messi's early career came in a match against Albacete. With just 2 minutes left in the game, he was subbed in, and in a matter of seconds, he nearly scored a spectacular goal. The crowd erupted in joy, but alas, the flag was raised, declaring it offside. Yet, Messi didn't give up. He soon replicated the same incredible move, this time with success, creating a moment for the ages.

In the summer, Messi took part in the Under-20 World Cup, showcasing his brilliance. Despite starting as a substitute due to stamina issues, he worked tirelessly to excel. He pushed his limits and became the top scorer of the tournament. Argentina emerged as champions, and Messi's star continued to rise.

Back in Barcelona, Messi became a first-team regular under the guidance of their new coach, Pep Guardiola. This was a turning point in Messi's career. He began to shine even brighter, setting the stage for unforgettable moments.

In his first full season as a regular, Messi scored his first Champions League goal with a remarkable chip shot. He continued to deliver impressive performances, and by January, he embarked on a goal-scoring streak, netting six goals in seven matches.

With the support of his teammates like Andres Iniesta and Xavi, Messi helped Barcelona win many trophies – La Liga titles, Copa del Rey, and even the prestigious Champions League. He became the heart and soul of the team, breaking records left and right. In 2012, he did the impossible by scoring 91 goals in a single year.

The UEFA Champions League brought Messi face-to-face with Cristiano Ronaldo for the first time, setting the stage for an epic rivalry. However, Barcelona lost that match. Messi's dedication and hard work led to his debut for the Argentina national team, although it didn't go as planned. He was sent off just minutes after coming on.

With each match, Messi continued to set records and achieve new heights. He took home his first Ballon D'Or, solidifying his status as the best player in the world. However, a formidable challenge emerged in the form of Cristiano Ronaldo, who joined Real Madrid, setting the stage for an intense rivalry.

Despite this rivalry, Messi kept getting better. He scored goals with ease, displaying incredible skills and making the impossible seem effortless. His magical performances took Barcelona to new heights, winning titles and the hearts of soccer fans worldwide.

In the following seasons, Messi's talent knew no bounds. He kept improving, dazzling the world with his goals, assists, and creativity. Even when faced with tough opponents like Chelsea and Inter Milan, Messi's brilliance shone through.

As Messi reached new heights, he continued to break records. He tied Ronaldo's record for the most goals in a Barcelona season. Their rivalry was legendary, and they constantly pushed each other to new heights.

But despite their on-field battles, Messi and Ronaldo always showed respect and friendship off the pitch. They even starred in a Louis Vuitton campaign together, playing chess and capturing the world's attention.

Messi wasn't just a star for his club; he was a hero for his country too. He often drew comparisons to the legendary Diego Maradona, especially after his stunning goals and performances for Argentina. He made his debut for the national team in 2005 and became their youngest player to appear in the World Cup in 2006.

In 2021, Messi led Argentina to victory in the Copa America, ending a 28-year-long drought. And then, in the 2022 World Cup, he guided his team to another triumph, lifting the coveted trophy and earning the Golden Ball as the tournament's best player.

As we reach the present day, Messi's story is still being written. His legacy as one of the greatest soccer players of all time is secure, and the world eagerly awaits the next chapter of his incredible journey.

The story of Lionel Messi teaches us an important lesson: that success doesn't come from luck or magic. It comes from hard work, determination, and a burning desire to achieve your dreams. Messi had his fair share of health issues, financial difficulties, and rejections. But he never gave up. He fought for his dreams and worked hard day in and day out.

There's no secret to his success – it's all about the effort you're willing to put in. As Messi himself says, "I start early and I stay late, day after day, year after year." It took him 17 years and 114 days to become an overnight success.

So, whatever your dream may be, remember that you have to work hard, make sacrifices, and never give up. Start today, work on your dreams, and who knows – maybe one day you'll be the hero of your own incredible success story.

In a small island called Madeira, there lived a young boy named Cristiano Ronaldo. Cristiano came from a very humble family, and life wasn't easy for them. His dad worked as a gardener but had troubles with alcohol, and sadly, in the year 2005, he passed away from liver failure. His mom, a hardworking cook and cleaning lady, did her best to provide hot meals for the family. Young Cristiano grew up in a humble background, and his family's financial situation was very tight.

Cristiano's childhood was filled with challenges. There were no fancy toys, and Christmas presents were rare in their home. He shared a room with his brother and two sisters, while his parents slept in another. But amidst the struggles, there was one thing that brought a smile to his face - a soccer ball. Whenever there was a ball around, Cristiano could forget about all the difficulties and focus on becoming the best.

Sometimes, he and his friends would visit a local burger shop to ask for leftover food. But you know what they all had in common? Their love for soccer! They spent most of their time playing the spirited game on the streets of their town, using a ball made of rags.

When he was just eight years old, Cristiano began playing for Andorinha, his very first soccer club. Even at such a young age, his talent was evident, and his hard work was impressive. At the age of 11, Ronaldo's skills caught the eye of Sporting Club in Portugal. People knew he was talented, but some said he was too small and skinny. Cristiano didn't like hearing that. "It's true I was skinny, I had no muscle," he admitted, "so I made a decision at 11 years old. I knew I had a lot of talent, but I decided that I was going to work harder than everybody."

Late at night, he would sneak out of the dormitory to work out. Cristiano got bigger and faster, and when he stepped onto the field, those who used to whisper about his size now watched in awe.

One of the toughest moments in Cristiano's life was leaving Madeira to join the Lisbon soccer academy. "Football gave me everything, but it also took me far away from home before I was really ready," he said.

At age 15, Cristiano was playing for Sporting Lisbon when his soccer career almost ended before it began. He was diagnosed with a heart condition that made his heart race, even when he wasn't running. He had to undergo heart surgery to fix the problem. But Cristiano Ronaldo is not one to give up easily. He chose to have the surgery. Thankfully, it was successful. After the successful surgery, he could finally run, practice, and focus on his dream.

All that hard work began to pay off. Cristiano became a remarkable player, outperforming everyone. And when he turned 16, he became eligible to play professionally. That's when Coach Laszlo Boloni took notice and helped Cristiano's career take off in the Portuguese league.

Then, on August 6, 2003, destiny knocked on Cristiano's door. He played a friendly match with Manchester United, showcasing his incredible skills and tactics. The Manchester United players were so impressed that they asked their manager, Sir Alex Ferguson, to sign Cristiano. A few days later, Cristiano Ronaldo became the first Portuguese player to join Manchester United and the most expensive teenager signed in history!

Cristiano Ronaldo signed a £15 million contract with Manchester United, becoming the first Portuguese player to join the team. Sir Alex Ferguson, the team's manager, believed in Cristiano's talents so much that he gave him the number seven jersey.

In 2009, Cristiano made a big move from Manchester United to Real Madrid for a record £94 million, making him the most expensive soccer player in history at that time. After almost a decade with Real Madrid, he signed a four-year contract with Juventus for a transfer fee of €100 million, the highest ever for a player over 30 years old.

Throughout his career, Cristiano Ronaldo won 34 trophies, including league titles, European Cups, and European Championship. But he, like everyone else, faced difficulties, failures, and disappointments along the way. What made him different was his incredible focus, hard work, and determination.

"I'm not a perfectionist, but I like to feel that things are done well," Cristiano said. "More important than that, I feel an endless need to learn, to improve, to evolve. It is my conviction that there are no limits to learning and that it can never stop, no matter what our age."

No matter the obstacles and setbacks, Cristiano Ronaldo never gave up. "We don't want to tell our dreams; we want to show them," he declared.

So, what does "never giving up" really mean? It means believing in yourself, no matter the circumstances. Cristiano Ronaldo always believed in himself, even when times were tough. He overcame a heart condition and countless challenges to become one of the greatest soccer players in the world. When you truly believe in yourself, you become invincible.

The desire to become great is universal, but only a few put in the time, work, sweat, and effort to achieve greatness. Cristiano Ronaldo's story teaches us that talent matters, but dedication matters even more. If you want to achieve greatness, strive to be the best version of yourself, and never give up on your dreams.

A young boy from Travagliato, just outside Milan, who was initially rejected by Inter Milan. But fate had other plans for him. AC Milan's youth academy welcomed him with open arms, and it wasn't long before he became a legend. So, there you have it, the beginnings of Franco Baresi's incredible journey.

Franco Baresi's journey to becoming a legend of AC Milan and Italian football began in 1978 when, as a 17-year-old, he joined the club's youth academy. Standing at just 5 feet 9 inches, Baresi wasn't the tallest player on the field, but what he lacked in height, he made up for in heart and exceptional playing ability. He was strong, fast, could jump with the best of them, and had an endless reserve of stamina. But it wasn't just his physical attributes that made him special; it was his incredible footballing mind.

Franco Baresi was more than just a defender; he was a master of the art of defending. His positioning was impeccable, and he had the uncanny ability to anticipate his opponent's every move. Baresi preferred to prevent attacks through his impeccable positioning, and it was rare to see him committing fouls or making tackles.

But when he did have to make a tackle, he was as precise as a surgeon. His tackling was clean, and he had perfect timing. He rarely found himself in trouble with referees, receiving just three red cards in his illustrious career.

One of the most remarkable aspects of Baresi's game was his composure on the ball. He could control the game from the back with his precise passing and ball control, often rivaling the skills of midfielders. Baresi's technique was world-class, and he had the ability to launch accurate long-range passes to initiate attacks.

Baresi's versatility was another feather in his cap. He could play as a ball-playing center-back or a sweeper. His ball-playing abilities were a testament to his all-around skills. Paolo Maldini himself admired Baresi's play, acknowledging that he was the best defender he had ever seen.

Baresi's journey started in 1978 when he joined AC Milan's first team as a 17-year-old. From there, he never looked back. He was part of a Milan squad that included legendary names. In his debut season, they secured the Scudetto by conceding just 19 goals in 30 games. This was a sign of things to come.

However, Milan faced turbulent times in the early '80s, suffering relegation to Serie B due to a match-fixing scandal. Despite these setbacks, Baresi's reputation remained untarnished. He continued to represent Italy in major tournaments, including the 1980 Euros and the 1982 World Cup, where Italy emerged victorious. Throughout these challenges, Baresi's loyalty to Milan remained steadfast. He stayed with the club and was rewarded with the captain's armband at the young age of 22.

Throughout these changes and additions, one thing remained constant—Franco Baresi's presence in the heart of Milan's defense. His leadership, intelligence, and unparalleled defensive skills made him an enduring legend in the world of soccer.

Imagine a time when teams focused on scoring just one goal and then dedicated the rest of the match to protecting that lead. Paolo Maldini was a master of this art, and he struck fear into the hearts of his opponents like no one else. Let's delve deeper into the incredible soccer career of Paolo Maldini.

Paolo Maldini came from a family deeply rooted in soccer. His father, Cesare Maldini, was a Milan legend and the former captain of the team that won the club's first European Cup. So, naturally, there were high expectations for Paolo. But little did anyone know just how extraordinary he would become. Paolo made his debut for AC Milan's first team when he was just 16 years old.

Imagine being just 16 years old and stepping onto the field for AC Milan's first team. Paolo Maldini did just that. Some may have thought he was there due to nepotism, considering his father Cesare Maldini's legendary status and captaincy of Milan's first-ever European Cup-winning team. However, it didn't take long for everyone to realize that Paolo was no mere beneficiary of his father's legacy. He was destined for greatness in his own right.

Maldini's debut at such a tender age was a testament to his extraordinary talent and skill. He was thrust into a world where experienced defenders grappled with some of the world's finest attackers, and yet he held his own. AC Milan was in the process of building a soccer dynasty, and Paolo Maldini was a crucial cornerstone of that grand plan.

What set Paolo Maldini apart from other defenders was his unique approach to the game. While many believed that tackling was the primary duty of a defender, Maldini had a different philosophy. He famously said, "If I have to make a tackle, then I have already made a mistake." For him, defense was about positioning, anticipation, and interceptions – all the qualities that prevented a situation from escalating into a tackle.

Despite his youthful appearance, Paolo Maldini possessed a mature and physically imposing presence on the field. He could outmuscle and outwit even seasoned players, and he did it with such finesse that he rarely found himself in the referee's book. Over the course of his remarkable 25-year career, he received just three red cards. His tackling was precise, and his timing was impeccable.

But Maldini's real genius lay in his ability to mark opponents. He had an uncanny knack for reading their movements, anticipating their actions, and shutting down their options. He was like a chess grandmaster playing against novices, dictating the flow of the game and frustrating his opponents to no end.

Yet Paolo Maldini wasn't merely a defensive juggernaut. He was a complete player. His composure on the ball, even under intense pressure, was remarkable. He had the passing accuracy, ball control, and vision of a midfielder. In fact, Ronaldinho, one of soccer's most skillful players, once praised Maldini for his incredible abilities.

Franco Baresi, an AC Milan legend himself, once remarked on Maldini's exceptional abilities, saying, "He was very young, so I tried to give him some advice, but he needed very little. He was already a great player."

Maldini's versatility extended beyond his defensive duties. He could deliver precise crosses, adding an attacking dimension to his game. Over the course of his career, he contributed to around 33 goals. His stamina allowed him to defend relentlessly while supporting his team on the counter-attack.

His ability to seamlessly transition from defense to attack made him a rare gem in the soccer world.

During his prime, Paolo Maldini was not just a defender; he was the most feared defender in the world. Even the most talented players dreaded facing him. To truly grasp Maldini's greatness, envision watching highlights of him defending against legendary figures like Ronaldo and Zidane. He made these footballing giants appear ordinary, a testament to his extraordinary abilities.

Paolo Maldini's career was defined by unwavering consistency. He dedicated nearly a quarter of a century to AC Milan, where he served as a leader, a symbol of composure, and a passionate defender.

The '87-'88 season saw Milan reclaim the Serie A title, and their defense was virtually impenetrable, conceding only 14 goals. This was just the beginning of their dominance. Over the next two seasons, they won the Champions League, solidifying their status as a soccer powerhouse.

The defensive lineup of Paolo Maldini, Franco Baresi, Alessandro Costacurta, Mauro Tassotti, and Giovanni Galli became legendary. This solid defense is often regarded as one of the best in soccer history.

In the soccer world, few players achieve the status of legends, but Paolo Maldini and Franco Baresi undoubtedly belong to that elite group. Their loyalty to AC Milan, their incredible defensive skills, and their impact on the sport make them immortal figures in soccer history. They are not just legendary; they are the stuff of soccer legends.

Paolo Maldini embodied the qualities of a legendary defender: intelligence, anticipation, positioning, and timing. He formed the bedrock of Milan's soccer dynasty and left an indelible mark on the sport. When ranking the all-time great defenders,

Paolo Maldini unquestionably stands at the summit, and his impact on the world of soccer will be celebrated for generations to come.

Let's step into the incredible story of Ronaldinho! Our adventure begins on March 21st, 1980, in a favela in Porto Alegre, Brazil. In this bustling neighborhood, a baby boy named Ronaldo de Assis Moreira was born. However, unlike most babies, Ronaldinho's arrival didn't bring immediate joy. He was born into a challenging environment, surrounded by drugs and gangs.

Ronaldinho grew up in a close-knit family with his brother Roberto and sister Deise. The family lived in a simple wooden house. Despite their tight finances, Ronaldinho's dad had not one but two jobs to make ends meet. During the week, he worked as a welder, and on the weekends, he oversaw the parking lot at the Gremio stadium, the local soccer club that held a special place in their hearts.

From a young age, Ronaldinho followed in his brother's footsteps, and he did so with a soccer ball at his feet. He spent every spare moment playing the beautiful game, and he couldn't imagine a life without it. He once said, "I think about soccer all the time. I live for soccer. I love spending my time with the ball. Without a ball, I'd be nearly dead. It's my entire life."

Thanks to soccer, Ronaldinho found moments of happiness that overshadowed the challenges around him. Seeing his passion, his father decided to sign him up for his first soccer club. That's when "Ronaldinho" was born, a nickname given to him by his teammates. They added "inho" to his name, which means "small" in Portuguese. Because he was one of the tiniest kids in his youth soccer club. And that name, "Ronaldinho," stuck with him throughout his entire career.

But don't let his size fool you; it was actually an advantage. Ronaldinho knew he couldn't rely on physical strength alone, so he developed dazzling skills and lightning-fast agility to outmanoeuvre his opponents.

When he wasn't at school, Ronaldinho could be found playing soccer. And when his friends grew tired, he turned to his loyal companion, his dog, Bumbum. Ronaldinho used to dribble past Bumbum to improve his ball-handling skills. He once said, "When I was little, my father made me work on my shooting, then my dog became my best playmate. He was the most faithful. He never got annoyed at being dribbled as long as he had a ball at his feet."

At the age of eight, Ronaldo's life took a devastating turn. After returning from a soccer game, he found his family gathered in the kitchen. At first, he thought they were celebrating his older brother Roberto's 18th birthday, but then he noticed his mother crying. Roberto took his younger brother into the bathroom and broke the heartbreaking news: "Dad is gone; he died."

Ronaldinho couldn't comprehend it. To him, his father was a hero, invincible. This loss would have crushed many, but Ronaldinho was made of stern stuff. Although he no longer had his father by his side, he had his older brother Roberto, who became his guiding light.

During these difficult times, Ronaldinho never lost his smile—a trait he inherited from his father. He drew strength from his family's unwavering support and his father's teachings. His father had always encouraged him to play his way and to be himself. And that's precisely what Ronaldinho did.

Despite facing criticism and doubts about his unconventional playing style, Ronaldinho remained true to himself. He once said, "I like to invent, to surprise. It's an obsession, like always having a ball at my side. I like to do unexpected things, to not know what will happen in the next three seconds. Football is that; it's instinct, and that's how I'll continue to play."

At the age of 13, Ronaldinho had his first big moment. In a game against a local team, his team won 23-0! And guess who scored all 23 goals? That's right, it was Ronaldinho. Imagine how embarrassed the other team must have felt. It was like playing a video game on easy mode with Ronaldinho on the field.

In July 1994, during the World Cup celebration after Brazil defeated Italy in the final, Ronaldinho realized that soccer was more than just a game. It was a source of immense joy and unity for people. At that moment, he made a promise to himself: he would become a world champion.

When Ronaldinho turned 18, he embarked on a journey with Gremio. Three years later, he set off to Paris Saint-Germain, discovering European soccer and mesmerizing fans with his extraordinary skills.

In 2002, Ronaldinho's childhood dream came true when he became a World Cup champion with Brazil. He was now a national hero, a symbol of triumph over adversity. His journey from poverty to the top of the soccer world was an inspiration to many.

In 2003, Barcelona came calling, outbidding Manchester United to sign Ronaldinho for 30 million euros. The 2004-2005 season was magical for Ronaldinho. Barcelona won La Liga, and he scored 13 goals and had 16 assists in 42 games. It was his best season yet, and he won another FIFA World Player of the Year award. In total, Ronaldinho scored 313 goals in 816 games throughout his career.

But life had its challenges in store for Ronaldinho. His mother, Dona, whom he admired for her strength and joy, passed away. Her death was another painful test, but it only made Ronaldinho stronger. He understood that death was simply a passage to another place.

He's shown us that passion is more important than anything else and that, with love and dedication, anything is possible.

And through all the hardships and challenges he's faced, he has never lost that infectious smile.

So, remember, no matter where you come from or what challenges life throws your way, keep your passion alive, and keep smiling. Just like Ronaldinho, you can overcome anything and leave your mark on the world.

In a small town in Brazil, there lived a boy who would grow up to become one of the greatest soccer players the world had ever seen. Little did the world know that this boy would grow up to be the greatest soccer player of all time, earning the nickname "The King" and "The Black Pearl." His name was Pelé, and his journey to stardom was nothing short of remarkable.

Pelé was born on October 23, 1940, in Brazil. His parents were Dondinho and Celeste. His father had a passion for soccer, and his mother was an actor, but they lived in poverty. To help his family, young Pelé took up odd jobs as a child.

Pele's journey to soccer stardom began in humble surroundings. When his family moved to Bauru City, young Pele discovered his passion for soccer. He didn't even have a real soccer ball to practice with, so he used stuffed socks as a makeshift one. Can you imagine that? Stuffed socks helping him become a soccer legend!

Now, let's talk about his name. Pele's real name was Edson Arantes do Nascimento, but his friends gave him the nickname Pele. Well, it all started when he mispronounced a Brazilian player's name, Bile. His friends playfully teased him by calling him Pele, and even though he didn't like it at first, the name stuck.

From an early age, Pelé's father taught him the art of soccer. He played for various amateur teams in his youth, displaying a natural talent that set him apart. Under the guidance of his coach, Waldemar de Brito, Pelé joined the Bauru Athletic Club juniors and led the team to three consecutive victories from 1954 to 1956.

In June 1956, Pelé's life took a major turn when he signed a contract with Santos FC, a professional soccer club. He played his first professional game in September of that year, and in that game, he scored his first professional goal against Corinthians Santo Andre.

By 1957, Pelé became a regular in the team, and his skills were earning him recognition. He made his debut for the national team of Brazil in July 1957, playing his first international game against Argentina. Although Brazil lost the match 2-1, Pelé scored his first international goal.

The year 1958 was a turning point for Pelé. He achieved remarkable success, scoring 58 goals in the Campeonato Paulista, a top-flight professional league in Brazil. But his biggest triumph came in the 1958 World Cup, where, as a teenager, he broke numerous records and scored six goals in four matches.

In the 1962 World Cup, Pelé battled injuries but remained a key player for Brazil. However, it was the 1966 World Cup that brought pain. Persistent fouling by the opposition, particularly the Bulgarians, led to Brazil's early exit from the tournament.

The 1970 World Cup marked Pelé's last appearance on the grand stage. He played a vital role, contributing to 14 of the 19 goals Brazil scored in the tournament. Brazil emerged as World Cup champions, and Pelé was named the Player of the Tournament.

After retiring in 1971 from international matches, Pelé continued his club career. In 1974, he retired from Santos after 19 seasons but came out of semi-retirement to play for the New

York Cosmos, leading the club to victory in the 1977 North American Soccer League championship.

Throughout his career, Pele scored more than 1,000 goals! That's like scoring a goal every single day for almost three years. He also became the first soccer player to become a millionaire, all thanks to sponsorship deals and his rising fame.

And that is the incredible rags-to-riches story of the great soccer legend, Pele. From practicing with stuffed socks to winning World Cups and capturing hearts worldwide, he's a true inspiration to all soccer lovers!

Despite the challenges he faced on and off the field, Pelé's legacy as one of the greatest soccer players of all time endures. His famous words, "If you are first, you are first. If you are second, you are nothing," continue to inspire countless young soccer players around the world.

ROBERTO CARLOS

In a small town in Brazil called Sao Paulo, a young boy named Roberto Carlos was born. He would grow up to become one of the greatest soccer players the world had ever seen, known for his incredible free kicks and unmatched skills. When he stepped onto the soccer field, he played with a fierce determination that set him apart from most other players.

But Roberto's journey to soccer stardom wasn't easy. He came from a very poor family, and at the age of 12, he had to start working to help support his parents. Despite the hardships, his heart belonged to soccer. He played whenever he could, even using a makeshift ball.

When he was just 19 years old, Roberto signed with a Brazilian club called Atlético Mineiro, and this marked the beginning of his remarkable journey. The team went on a tour of Europe, where Roberto got to showcase his skills on a big stage. He played in Spain and caught the eye of talent scouts, opening up new opportunities for him.

Back in Brazil, he joined an even bigger club called Palmeiras and helped them win two league titles. But Roberto Carlos knew he was destined for more, and he faced a tough decision.

Should he join Aston Villa in the prestigious Premier League or Inter Milan in Italy? Both teams wanted him, but he chose Inter Milan.

In his debut match for Inter Milan, Roberto Carlos scored a goal from a free kick, proving that he was the real deal. However, there was a problem. The coach wanted him to play in midfield, not as a left-back, which is where Roberto felt he belonged. This led to disagreements, and he decided to leave Inter Milan.

What Roberto Carlos did next changed soccer forever. Before him, defenders were expected to stay back and defend the goal. But Roberto was different. He was fast, fit, and incredibly skilled with the ball. He could score goals, take free kicks, and assist in scoring opportunities. He showed the world that full-backs could be attacking threats too.

Then came the golden era at Real Madrid, where Roberto Carlos played from 1996 to 2007. He was part of the "Galácticos," a team filled with legends like David Beckham, Luís Figo, Zinedine Zidane, and Ronaldo. He joined the club within 24 hours of becoming available, and his impact was immediate. Real Madrid won three Champions League titles and four La Liga titles during his time there.

In 2003, during the famous El Clásico match against Barcelona, Roberto Carlos scored a stunning free kick that helped Real Madrid beat Barcelona for the first time in 20 years. His salary was a whopping 10 million per year, and he earned every cent with his incredible skills.

But what really made Roberto Carlos a legend was his unforgettable free kick in 1997. It was during a tournament in France, and the odds were against him. The free kick was 35 meters away from the goal, and nobody expected him to score. But he did. With the outside of his left foot, he curled the ball into the net, and it seemed to defy gravity. Scientists even had to study how the ball moved because it was so incredible.

Roberto Carlos also shone on the biggest stage of them all, the World Cup. In 1998, he helped Brazil reach the final, and in 2002, he was a key part of the team that won the World Cup. It was the pinnacle of his career, and he called it a dream come true.

After retiring from international soccer, Roberto Carlos still loved the game. He even played in a small town in England, where lucky local players got to share the field with a World Cup winner. It was a reminder of his humble beginnings, playing on makeshift fields while working and going to school to support his family.

Roberto Carlos's legacy in soccer is undeniable. He was a consistent and flamboyant player, known for his incredible dribbling, explosive speed, and powerful shots. His trophy cabinet boasts numerous titles, including Copa America, Confederations Cup, Champions League, and World Cup.

His legacy as a left-back, often hailed as one of the best in history, is cemented in the annals of soccer. With his iconic free-kicks and indomitable spirit, Roberto Carlos's name will forever be synonymous with greatness.

And that, my young friends, is the incredible story of Roberto Carlos, a soccer legend who changed the game, one gravity-defying free kick at a time. His journey from poverty to stardom serves as an inspiration to all soccer lovers around the world.

RONALDO NAZÁRIO

There was a soccer superstar known as Cristiano Ronaldo. But before Cristiano, there was another Ronaldo who made the name famous – Ronaldo Luís Nazário de Lima. He's often called the "original Ronaldo," and during his incredible career, he went by the nickname "The Phenomenon." Let's dive into his story.

He had a passion for soccer that burned brighter than the Brazilian sun. His mother, Sonia, fondly recalled those days. "I always found him on the streets, playing with his friends" she would say with a chuckle.

When Ronaldo was just 11 years old, his parents went their separate ways. This unexpected change in his life led Ronaldo to leave school behind. The world outside was tough, especially for an 11-year-old, but he had his escape and his savior: soccer.

Soccer became his sanctuary. No matter the circumstances, Ronaldo's dedication and passion for the game shone brightly. It was as if the soccer gods had chosen him. At the tender age of 12, he joined a local futsal team called Social Ramos.

On his debut season, Ronaldo scored a jaw-dropping 166 goals, including one unforgettable match where he netted 11 out of his team's 12 goals. Imagine being on the opposing team, watching in awe as he weaved through defenders like a magician.

Futsal, with its tight spaces and fast-paced action, was where Ronaldo honed his skills. The narrow alleyways and uneven pavement of his childhood forced him to master ball control and develop an incredibly soft touch.

One day, Brazilian legend Jairzinho, a hero from the 1970 World Cup, spotted young Ronaldo. Jairzinho saw something special in the kid, something different. He knew that Ronaldo belonged with the best, and he wasn't about to let him slip away.

Jairzinho recommended the 16-year-old Ronaldo join his former club, Cruzeiro. But Ronaldo had always dreamt of playing for Flamengo, the team he had supported since childhood. Unfortunately, Flamengo didn't see the potential in him and didn't offer him a chance. So, Jairzinho pulled some strings and convinced Cruzeiro to sign the young prodigy.

At the incredibly young age of 16, Ronaldo made his professional debut for Cruzeiro. Just think, when most of us were 16, we were playing video games, not facing fully grown professionals on a soccer pitch.

It didn't take long for Ronaldo to capture the nation's attention. He scored five goals in a single game, leaving even seasoned footballers in disbelief. Former Brazilian captain Cafu remembered the first time he saw Ronaldo play, saying, "He was still a kid. It was in a game where he ended up scoring five goals."

Ronaldo proved he was a phenomenon. Flamengo soon realized their grave mistake as Ronaldo, at 16, scored a remarkable 44 goals in 47 games over two seasons for Cruzeiro. He helped his club, which wasn't considered a real contender, win the Brazilian Cup.

As a 17-year-old, Ronaldo was called up to join the Brazilian national team for the 1994 World Cup. Brazil would go on to win that tournament, even though Ronaldo didn't play a minute. But being part of that victorious squad, surrounded by legends, was a priceless experience.

Ronaldo's journey in Europe began when he was just 18 years old. His first stop was the Netherlands, where he played for PSV Eindhoven. He was unstoppable! In two short years, he scored an incredible 54 goals in 57 games.

After his Dutch adventure, Ronaldo made a move to Barcelona. During his one season there, he lit up the field, helping Barcelona win the Copa del Rey and the Cup Winners' Cup. He scored a jaw-dropping 47 goals in just 49 games and even won the Ballon d'Or, making him the youngest player ever to receive that prestigious award.

Next up was a transfer to Inter Milan in Italy. In his first season, Ronaldo's brilliance led Inter Milan to victory in the UEFA Cup. He was also a key part of the Brazil national team that reached the World Cup final. Ronaldo had previously been part of Brazil's World Cup-winning squad in 1994, even though he didn't play much.

But then came a moment of disaster. Just before the 1998 World Cup final against France, Ronaldo suffered a convulsive fit. Although doctors cleared him to play, he was far from his usual self, and Brazil lost 3-0.

After that heartbreaking event, Ronaldo faced a series of knee injuries that kept him away from the field for nearly three years. Some feared his career might be over, but Ronaldo wasn't ready to give up.

In an incredible comeback story, he made it back in time for the 2002 World Cup. It was like a real-life fairy tale! Ronaldo not only returned but finished as the tournament's top scorer, helping Brazil win the World Cup.

Ronaldo then spent four years at Real Madrid, scoring an astonishing 104 goals in 177 games. Although he had a remarkable individual record, Real Madrid only won one La Liga title during that time.

After a brief stint at AC Milan, Ronaldo returned to Brazil at the age of 33. While he might not have had the same explosive speed he had in his younger days, he was still a beloved figure in the soccer world.

However, his knee problems eventually caught up with him, robbing him of his explosive pace. But even after that setback, he was still an excellent goal-scorer. He adapted his game and continued to be a clinical finisher, displaying an exquisite first touch.

In 2011, Ronaldo announced his retirement. His body had endured too much – injuries, surgeries, and the relentless march of time. But he remained an icon, one of the greatest players ever to grace the beautiful game.

Ronaldo's story serves as a reminder that even the most incredible talents can face setbacks. His dedication, skill, and indomitable spirit continue to inspire soccer fans around the world. He may have left the pitch, but his legacy as a true phenomenon lives on, forever etched in the annals of soccer history. And as Lionel Messi once said, "He was my hero." If Messi calls you his hero, you must be something truly special.

In the world of soccer, there was a player who changed the game forever. You might have heard of Pele and Maradona, but in Europe, there was another name that shines just as brightly.

In the year 1947, a baby boy was born into a loving family. Little did they know, this child was destined to fall in love with soccer, thanks to the influence of his father. But life took a tragic turn when, just four years later, his father passed away from a heart attack. This young boy's name was Johan Cruyff.

Johan Cruyff was not your ordinary soccer player. From a young age, his skills stood out like a shooting star in the night sky. When he was just 10 years old, playing with the kids in his neighborhood, an Ajax youth coach spotted him. Without hesitation, he offered Johan a spot in the club's youth program, knowing he had found someone truly special.

By the time he was 17, Johan Cruyff made his debut in the men's team for Ajax. At that time, Ajax was struggling, but Johan was about to change their fortunes. In his very first season as a starter, he scored 25 goals in 23 matches, helping

Ajax become champions. Yes, you read that right, 25 goals in his first season!

Cruyff continued to shine. He scored a remarkable 41 goals in 41 appearances, securing another league title and a Dutch Cup. He was unstoppable. And the next season, he scored 34 goals and had 40 assists in 40 appearances – that's nearly a goal or an assist every game!

But Johan Cruyff didn't stop there. In 1969-1970, he helped Ajax win another league title and a Dutch Cup, scoring 33 goals and providing 34 assists. He was not just a goal machine; he was a creator too. And did you know he's the only player to score at least 30 goals in a season while also having more assists than anyone else?

In the 1970-1971 season, Johan Cruyff led Ajax to European glory, winning the European Cup. It was a big deal, like winning today's Champions League. He scored 27 goals, and Ajax was on top of the world.

But what made Cruyff truly unique was his style of play. He could switch effortlessly between midfield and attack, pressing the opposition like Messi does today. His skill and versatility led Ajax to an unbeaten run of 46 games in two seasons!

After leaving Ajax and playing for Barcelona, Johan Cruyff continued to dazzle fans with his skills. He won La Liga in 1974 and the Copa del Rey in 1978, scoring 85 goals in 227 appearances. And remember the famous Cruyff turn? He invented that move during the 1974 World Cup!

Cruyff's impact wasn't limited to the field; he became a legendary manager too. He coached Ajax and later Barcelona, where he laid the foundations for their future success. He introduced innovations like the 4-3-3 formation and nurtured talents like Pep Guardiola. He left an indelible mark on Barcelona, where he won multiple La Liga titles and the Champions League.

Johan Cruyff may have left us in 2016, but his legacy lives on. He changed the way soccer is played, leaving an indelible mark on the beautiful game. His name will be spoken for generations to come, reminding us of the greatness he brought to soccer.

Johan Cruyff's impact on soccer cannot be overstated. He was not just a player; he was a pioneer, an innovator, and a legend. His influence lives on in the way the game is played today.

And that's the story of Johan Cruyff, a soccer legend whose influence on the game will never fade away and continues to inspire the hearts of soccer fans around the world.

FRANZ
BECKENBAUER

There was a soccer hero named Franz Beckenbauer. He wasn't just any hero; he earned his place through hard work and determination. A legendary figure named Gunter Netzer once said, "He's the hero of our nation." He achieved the incredible feat of becoming a world champion both as a player and as a manager.

Franz Anton Beckenbauer was born on September 11, 1945, right in the heart of post-war Munich. He started playing soccer with determination when he was just nine years old. Soccer has many positions, and some are more glamorous than others. Defense, where Franz played, often doesn't get the spotlight. But that didn't bother him. Out of all the Ballon d'Or awards given out (it's like the Oscars for soccer), only three defenders have ever won it. Franz was one of them, winning it twice!

Franz wasn't just a regular defender; he was a sweeper, also known as a libero. It's a fancy way of saying he had the freedom to roam all over the field. He could defend like a champion and playmake like a magician. His role was like a superhero on the soccer field.

Franz was known for his incredible game reading, athleticism, and technical skills. He could defend, carry the ball forward, pass, dribble, and shoot. He became the heart and soul of his teams, both in club and international matches.

Franz's soccer journey started in post-war Germany, where life was tough. But as a young boy, he found his passion: soccer. He played for local teams and dreamt of wearing the blue jersey of 1860 Munich. But one day, in a big tournament, something unexpected happened. He faced 1860 Munich in the finals, and a high-five to his face made him change his mind. Instead, he joined their city rivals, Bayern Munich.

Bayern Munich wasn't in the top league at the time, but that turned out to be a blessing. They built a young, talented team around Franz, and they finally made it to the Bundesliga, the top league in Germany.

In 1966, Franz played in the World Cup for Germany. It was an incredible tournament, but they fell short in the finals against England. Still, Franz stood out and was named the best young player of the tournament. His star was rising.

By 1968, he had earned the nickname "Der Kaiser" (The Emperor) and was leading Bayern Munich as their captain. He helped them win the Bundesliga and the European Cup multiple times. But he didn't stop there; he also led Germany to victory in the 1972 European Championship.

The crowning achievement came in 1974 when Franz captained the German national team to win the World Cup. In the final, he marked the Ballon d'Or winner Johan Cruyff out of the game. He was a true hero on the field.

Franz won two Ballon d'Or awards himself in 1972 and 1976, an incredible feat for a defender. But his success didn't end with Germany; he took his talents to America, playing for the New York Cosmos, where he won league titles.

He returned to Germany to play for Hamburg and continued to win the Bundesliga. But eventually, Franz hung up his boots, retiring at the age of 38. But his story didn't end there.

Franz Beckenbauer became a successful manager, leading Germany to the World Cup final in 1986 and winning it in 1990. He was one of the few to win the World Cup both as a player and a manager. Franz also became the president of Bayern Munich, where the club continued to thrive under his leadership.

Franz Beckenbauer's legacy in the world of soccer is unparalleled. He was a hero, a leader, and a game-changer. His story reminds us that with hard work, determination, and a passion for what you love, you can achieve greatness, no matter where you start. The Emperor of football left an indelible mark on the beautiful game, inspiring generations of soccer players and fans alike.

The story of Ferenc Puskás is a tale of soccer greatness that began in the midst of adversity. Puskás, one of the greatest goal scorers of all time, emerged from humble beginnings to become a legend in the world of soccer.

Ferenc Puskás was born in Budapest, Hungary, in 1927, during a time when the world was grappling with complicated historical events. His early connection to soccer was deeply rooted, as his father had been a coach and a professional player. As a teenager, Puskás displayed immense promise on the soccer field, scoring 24 goals in 51 appearances before even turning 18.

However, it wasn't until the 1945-1946 season, shortly after World War II, that Puskás truly caught the world's attention. At just 18 years old, he achieved something incredible by scoring an astonishing 36 goals in 34 appearances, averaging more than a goal per game. This was also the year he made his debut for the Hungarian national team, where he scored three goals in two appearances. Such remarkable achievements at such a young age were nothing short of extraordinary.

Puskás began his professional career at Kispest, a club where he continued to shatter goal-scoring records. In the 1946-1947 season, he netted 32 goals in 29 appearances, boasting a remarkable 1.10 goals-per-game ratio. The following year, he outdid himself with an unbelievable 50 goals in 30 appearances, with an astounding 1.56 goals-per-game ratio, making him the top goal scorer in Europe.

Puskás wasn't content with just one fantastic season. He followed it up with another outstanding performance, scoring 46 goals in 28 matches, an astonishing 1.64 goals-per-game ratio. Such consistent goal-scoring prowess was rarely seen in the soccer world.

Puskás wasn't just a goal-scoring machine; he possessed lightning-fast speed, even though he wasn't a physically imposing player. His strength, impeccable finishing skills, soft first touch, and incredible positioning made him a complete package on the field. His teammates admired him for his talent, and his opponents feared his goal-scoring ability.

In 1949, Hungary underwent significant political changes, falling under the influence of the Soviet Union and adopting a communist regime. This political shift had implications for soccer as well. Puskás's club, Kispest, was taken over by the Hungarian Ministry of Defense, becoming the Hungarian army team and later changing its name to Budapest Honvéd. This transformation allowed them to recruit the best Hungarian players, creating a dominant force in the country.

Puskas continued to shine, helping Budapest Honvéd win five Hungarian league titles. His goal-scoring records at the club were nothing short of incredible. In the 1949-1950 season, he scored 31 goals in 30 appearances, and the following year, he achieved an astounding 1.66 goals-per-game ratio with 25 goals in just 15 matches.

Puskás's fame grew internationally when he led Hungary to an Olympic gold medal in 1952. He was instrumental in Hungary's victory, scoring four goals, including one in the final. However, it was the match against England in 1953 that truly put Hungary on the world soccer map. Hungary defeated England 6-3, with Puskás delivering breathtaking goals that left a lasting impression.

Despite his immense success, Puskás faced personal challenges. In 1956, Hungary's political situation escalated, leading to the Hungarian Revolution. The government's handling of the soccer team changed, and Puskás and several of his Honvéd teammates sought to play for foreign leagues. Puskás found himself in Spain, joining Real Madrid in 1958 at the age of 31.

Remarkably, even at an age when most players would be past their prime, Puskás displayed incredible talent. In his first season with Real Madrid, he scored 25 goals in 34 appearances. The following season, he had the highest goal-scoring season of his career, netting 47 goals in 40 appearances. Puskás helped Real Madrid secure five consecutive La Liga titles, won another European Cup, and claimed several scoring titles.

Despite being physically past his prime, Puskás continued to defy expectations. He retired from professional soccer at the age of 39, leaving an incredible legacy. He ended his career with 625 goals in 629 appearances and scored 84 goals in 85 international matches throughout a 24-year career.

In recognition of his incredible career, FIFA named the award for the best goal of the year after him – the Puskás Award. Ferenc Puskás, "The Galloping Major," will forever be remembered as a soccer icon who defied the odds and left an indelible mark on the beautiful game.

Puskás's story is one of determination, resilience, and unwavering commitment to the sport he loved. His journey from adversity to greatness is a testament to the idea that hard work and dedication can overcome any obstacle. His legacy lives on as an inspiration to aspiring soccer players around the world, reminding them that age is no barrier to achieving greatness through passion, humility, and relentless effort.

ALFREDO DI STEFANO

There was a legendary player named Alfredo Di Stefano. He was born in Buenos Aires, Argentina, on July 4, 1926, and from a very young age, he fell in love with the beautiful game of soccer. His father, who had played professionally for River Plate, introduced him to the sport. Little did anyone know that this young boy would go on to become one of the greatest soccer players of all time.

As he grew older, Di Stefano's talent on the soccer field became more and more apparent. He started playing for local clubs and gained popularity for his incredible skills. When he turned old enough to play for a men's team in 1944, his father wrote a letter of recommendation to River Plate, his former club. But it wasn't just the letter that got him in; it was his impressive skills during the audition that earned him a spot on the team.

In a twist of fate, Di Stefano's first official match for River Plate was against their local rivals, Huracan. What happened during that match was truly remarkable. Di Stefano scored a goal just 10 seconds into the game, setting a record for the fastest goal ever scored in the Argentine Primera Division. This incredible feat caught the attention of everyone, including

Huracan, who now wanted to sign him away from River Plate. But Di Stefano's heart was set on playing for River Plate, the team his family supported and where his father had once played. This time, River Plate refused to let him go.

During his early days with River Plate, Di Stefano played as a winger, a position that didn't quite suit his unique playing style. However, his coach soon recognized his potential as a center forward, and Di Stefano's career took off from there. He adapted to his new role and became a goal-scoring sensation.

In his first full season as a forward, Di Stefano scored an astonishing 28 goals in 32 appearances, helping River Plate clinch the Argentinian league title. At just 21 years old, he was named the league's top scorer.

But the story doesn't end there. Di Stefano's talent didn't go unnoticed, and he earned a spot on Argentina's national team. He was the youngest player on the squad but quickly became a star during the 1947 Copa America. He scored six goals in seven appearances, including a memorable hat-trick against Colombia. Argentina won the tournament, and Di Stefano's name was etched in the history books.

However, one of the most intriguing moments of his time at River Plate happened in a match against their arch-rivals, Boca Juniors. In a move that would be like FC Barcelona's Messi playing as a goalkeeper in El Clasico, Di Stefano kept a clean sheet as a goalkeeper during that match. It was a testament to his versatility and skills.

After his time in Argentina, Di Stefano embarked on a journey to Colombia, where he played for Millonarios. During his time there, he continued to shine, scoring a remarkable 100 goals in 111 appearances. However, the Colombian league was not officially recognized by FIFA at the time, which led to a complicated situation for Di Stefano.

He even briefly played for the Colombian national team, although he never had Colombian citizenship or any formal affiliation with the country. To this day, FIFA doesn't recognize this period in Colombian football history, making it a unique and somewhat controversial chapter in Di Stefano's career.

In 1952, Di Stefano became the hottest target for European clubs. Two giants, Real Madrid and Barcelona, engaged in a fierce bidding war to secure his signature. However, the circumstances surrounding his transfer were far from ordinary. River Plate owned his rights for FIFA-affiliated leagues, while Colombia operated outside of FIFA's jurisdiction. A FIFA representative had to intervene to resolve the matter.

Ultimately, an agreement was reached that allowed Di Stefano to play for Real Madrid for one season, with the possibility of moving to Barcelona afterward. Barcelona later sold their rights to sign Di Stefano to Real Madrid after his sensational first season.

Di Stefano's debut season with Real Madrid was nothing short of spectacular. He scored 27 goals in 28 appearances, quickly becoming a fan favorite and catapulting Real Madrid to success. It was the start of a remarkable era for the club, with Di Stefano at the forefront.

His style of play was unconventional but utterly mesmerizing. While he possessed exceptional touch, finishing ability, and precise long-distance shots, Di Stefano was known for his versatility. He could be found all over the pitch, defending, leading counter-attacks, and even playing as a forward. His dribbling skills were legendary, leaving defenders in awe.

Under Di Stefano's leadership, Real Madrid went on to win multiple La Liga titles and consecutive Champions League titles. His impact on the club's success was immeasurable. He was a goal-scoring machine, consistently topping the charts as Europe's leading goal scorer.

In the 1956-57 season, Di Stefano had his most exceptional individual campaign. He scored a staggering 43 goals in 43 appearances, won his third La Liga title, and secured his third consecutive Champions League title. It was a season that would earn him his first Ballon d'Or, a well-deserved accolade.

Real Madrid's dominance in European football was cemented during this period, thanks in large part to Di Stefano. They became a global powerhouse, attracting fans and resources from all corners of the world. With his contributions, Real Madrid built better training facilities and had the financial means to make significant signings, ensuring their success for generations to come.

Di Stefano's impact wasn't limited to the field; it extended to the hearts of fans worldwide. He became a Spanish citizen and even helped Spain qualify for the 1962 World Cup. Unfortunately, an injury prevented him from facing Pele and Garrincha in what would have been an epic clash.

As Di Stefano entered his mid-thirties, his performance gradually declined, but he continued to win La Liga titles with Real Madrid. After an incredible 11 seasons with the club, he retired with two Ballon d'Or awards, five consecutive Champions League titles, and a legacy that would forever define Real Madrid's history.

In total, Di Stefano scored 308 goals in 396 appearances for Real Madrid over more than a decade. He scored a staggering 487 goals in 669 appearances throughout his 22-year career.

Alfredo Di Stefano wasn't just a soccer player; he was a legend, an icon, and the man who transformed Real Madrid into the colossal club we know today.

Zinedine Zidane, or Zizou as he's often called, had an incredible career in the world of soccer. Zidane's journey began in 1972 when he was born in Marseille, France. His parents had moved from Algeria to southern France, and Zinedine was the youngest of their five children. His father worked as a watchman, leaving for work in the evening and returning in the morning. Zidane often spoke about how his father's strong work ethic influenced him.

From a very young age, Zidane had a deep passion for soccer. He was a fan of the local team, Marseille, and he idolized players like Jean-Pierre Papin and Enzo Francescoli. In fact, he admired Francescoli so much that he named his own son Enzo.

At the age of fourteen, Zidane was scouted by Cannes, a soccer club. The scout who discovered him was amazed by how he could make the ball dance with his feet. Zidane was quickly brought into the club's academy and started working his way up through the youth ranks. However, there was one significant issue that threatened to hinder his progress.

Zidane had immense talent, but he also had a bit of a temper. He often reacted poorly when opponents fouled him, even getting sent off at times. His fiery nature even led to confrontations with spectators who insulted his family. Despite these challenges, Zidane's talent was undeniable.

In his first full season with the Cannes first team, they achieved an impressive fourth-place finish in Ligue 1. This was a remarkable achievement for a club of their size, and it got everyone talking about the young attacking midfielder who seemed to have an almost magical connection with the ball.

Zidane continued to earn praise over the years, and at one point, he was close to joining a Premier League club. Surprisingly, it wasn't one of the big names you'd expect. In 1992, he made a move to Bordeaux, a step up in his career. It didn't take long for him to prove that he could handle the challenge.

In the 1995-1996 season, Zidane helped Bordeaux reach the UEFA Cup final, although they narrowly lost to Bayern Munich. But that season, a big English club showed interest in him. Blackburn Rovers, managed by Kenny Dalglish, were eager to sign him. However, Jack Walker, the club's chairman, had a legendary response: "Why do you want to sign Zidane when we have Tim Sherwood?"

In 1996, Zidane joined Juventus, a club that had just won the Champions League. His arrival was seen as a move that could take Juventus to even greater heights. And indeed, it was. Zidane's debut season in Italy was spectacular. He was named Serie A Foreign Footballer of the Year as Juventus clinched the league title.

Zidane quickly formed a fantastic partnership with Alessandro Del Piero, another soccer star. Del Piero described Zidane as an extraordinary talent with a unique ability. However, Zidane's true breakthrough came on the international stage in 1998.

During the 1998 World Cup, as the host nation, France faced Brazil in the final. Zidane stepped onto the pitch with a mission. In a stunning performance, he scored two crucial goals, leading France to a resounding 3-0 victory. Zidane was not only a key player but also a national hero. He was voted into FIFA's all-star team of the tournament and won the prestigious Ballon d'Or.

Zidane's incredible journey continued as he moved to Real Madrid in 2001. In his debut season, he helped Real Madrid secure the Champions League trophy with a spectacular left-footed volley.

Zidane, known for his incredible dribbling, vision, and passing, was the creative force behind his teams. His style of play was often described as artistry on the pitch. Even though he didn't score as many goals as some of his contemporaries like Lionel Messi and Cristiano Ronaldo, his impact went far beyond statistics. He had the rare ability to control games and make the impossible look effortless.

One of Zidane's remarkable traits was his mental strength and character. He consistently performed in high-pressure situations and made a significant impact on the biggest stages. When Zlatan Ibrahimović said, "When Zidane stepped onto the pitch, the 10 other guys just suddenly got better," it summed up Zidane's ability to elevate his team.

While Zidane may not be in the same category as Messi, Ronaldo, Pelé, or Diego Maradona in the debate of the greatest of all time (GOAT), he certainly belongs to the next tier of soccer legends. He's often compared to Michel Platini, and they are considered the best French soccer players in history.

In the end, Zidane's legacy is more about the magic he brought to the game and his ability to shine when it mattered most. He may not have scored as many goals as others, but his impact on the world of soccer and his status as one of the all-time greats remain unquestionable.

Dani Alves hails from a tiny village called Juazeiro in Brazil. It's a place where life is hard, and people play soccer to escape the troubles of their daily lives. But this is where Dani's story begins. He was born into a family that didn't have much. His dad worked hard in the fields, and his family's home was small and humble.

When Dani was just ten years old, he was waking up in a tiny house with a mattress as thin as your little finger. His world smelled like damp soil, and outside, it was still dark. At 5:00 in the morning, while most kids were still sleeping, he was already out in the fields, helping his dad before school. He knew the value of hard work from a young age.

But Dani had a dream. When he was just six years old, he dreamt of playing in the World Cup. This was a boy who knew exactly what he wanted from life and was ready to chase that dream. His life was tough, but he was an extrovert, always playing and joking with everyone, always dreaming of something bigger.

Fast forward to the year 2001, and this young boy found himself starting for his first team. It only took him four minutes after stepping onto the pitch to make his mark. He gave an assist, and then another one after a short break. Before he was subbed off around the 16th minute, he even won a penalty for his team's third and final goal. It was like magic on the field!

Now, here's what makes Dani Alves extraordinary. Most Brazilian players spend years playing in Brazil before making the big leap to European football, but not him. He only played 30 matches in Brazil before catching the eye of Sevilla, a club in Spain. At first, they were a bit worried about spending big money on a 19-year-old right back, but they soon realized his talent was worth every penny.

In 2003, Dani Alves took part in the World Youth Cup and was named the third-best player in the tournament as Brazil won the trophy. It was clear that he was a rising star.

His first season at Sevilla wasn't perfect, and he didn't always play a full 90 minutes. But the next year, he became a frequent starter for the team. Sevilla was going through a dry spell without winning any trophies, but in 2006, things changed. With the arrival of other key players, Dani Alves finally lifted his first trophy in Spain – the UEFA Cup.

The real magic happened in the 2006-2007 season. Dani Alves helped Sevilla win not only the Copa del Rey but also revalidated their UEFA Cup title, becoming the second-ever team to win it consecutively. That summer, he took part in his first international tournament for Brazil, the Copa America. He played four matches, including the final against Argentina, where he scored a goal and set up another. Brazil won 3-0, and Dani Alves had his first international trophy.

This success made Dani Alves a sought-after player, and many clubs tried to sign him. But Sevilla held on for one more season before Barcelona finally managed to secure his services for a fee of 33 million euros. He instantly became a key player for Barcelona, starting almost every game and helping the team achieve the historic treble – winning La Liga, the Copa del Rey, and the Champions League.

Following this massive achievement, Barcelona went on to win the Club World Cup, with Dani Alves even assisting the winning goal in the final. He continued to shine in international competitions, taking part in the Intercontinental Cup for Brazil and making a mark by scoring a crucial free-kick goal.

His second season at Barcelona started on a high note as he won both the Spanish and European Super Cups, adding to his growing list of titles. Dani Alves played a pivotal role as Barcelona retained their La Liga title.

In 2010, he participated in his first-ever World Cup for Brazil, and although they got knocked out in the quarterfinals, Dani Alves continued to shine. He earned his first Ballon d'Or nomination that year.

The following season was just as successful, with Barcelona winning both La Liga and the Champions League again, defeating Manchester United in the final. Dani Alves was consistently excellent.

The years that followed brought domestic success for Barcelona and participation in another Confederations Cup, which Brazil won. Dani Alves continued to collect trophies and establish himself as one of the greatest right-backs of his generation.

In 2014, he played in the World Cup hosted by his own country, Brazil, although the tournament is most remembered for Germany's shocking 7-1 win over Brazil in the semifinals.

In the 2014-2015 season, Dani Alves and Barcelona won the treble again – La Liga, the Copa del Rey, and the Champions League. It was an incredible achievement.

However, despite his success, Dani Alves decided to leave Barcelona after posting a video that upset the club's board. He joined Juventus, where he almost won another treble in his single season there. Juventus won the league and cup, and Dani Alves played a crucial role in their journey to the Champions League final.

After leaving Juventus, he played for Paris Saint-Germain (PSG) for two years, where he added more trophies to his collection. Despite these seasons being less remarkable, he still managed to win.

Then came a significant moment in his career. Dani Alves returned to his childhood club, São Paulo FC, where he had always dreamed of playing. He even had the honor of captaining the national team, Brazil, for the first time. It was a special moment for him, and Brazil went on to win the tournament, giving Dani Alves his second Copa America trophy.

Currently, he still plays for São Paulo FC, and even though he hasn't won any more trophies, he continues to be a beloved figure in Brazilian football.

Dani Alves has not only been an incredible player but also an entertaining personality. He's known for his unique outfits at the Ballon d'Or ceremonies and the time he ate a banana thrown at him by a racist fan during a match. He's not just a great player; he's a symbol of resilience and joy on the field.

MICHEL PLATINI

Michel Platini, like many great French soccer players, had a unique and inspiring story. He was born to Italian parents who had fled their homeland after World War I. This made him a bit different from other French soccer stars, but his talent was undeniable.

During his teenage years, Platini had a dream. He wanted to join the prestigious Metz FC soccer team. However, his dreams took a hit when he suffered an injury that prevented him from joining the team. Later, after failing a medical test, it seemed like his soccer dreams might be over before they even began. But Platini was not one to give up easily.

He found his way to Nancy, a soccer club where his father served as a director. Initially, things were tough for him, but he quickly won the hearts of fans. Platini's big break came when he scored a hat-trick for the B team, earning a chance to play for the first team. However, his journey had its ups and downs.

In his first match for the first team, Platini faced adversity. He was spat on and pelted with objects thrown from the stands as a fight erupted. But he didn't let that deter him. In another match for the reserves, he suffered a severe injury that kept him away from the first team until May. However, when he finally got his opportunity, he scored two crucial goals against Lyon.

The following season, Platini became a regular starter for the first team. Yet, bad luck struck again as he broke his arm in two different places during a match against Nice, forcing him to watch Nancy get relegated from the sidelines.

But Platini's true potential began to shine through. In the following season, he scored a remarkable 30 goals in 43 matches, helping Nancy secure promotion. He even played a pivotal role in knocking out reigning champions Saint-Étienne from the French Cup.

Despite occasional struggles with injuries and military service obligations, Platini continued to rise. At just 20 years old, he achieved a hat trick against Marseille, showcasing his exceptional skills.

Then, something extraordinary happened. Platini and his team defied the odds and reached the final of the French Cup. Facing

Nice, Platini rose to the occasion, scoring the only goal and earning his first-ever trophy.

His journey continued to the 1978 World Cup. France's performance was a disappointment, and Platini faced criticism from fans after an early exit, despite his earlier brilliance against Italy. But Platini was not one to be deterred by setbacks.

After one more season at Nancy, Platini moved on to play for AS Saint-Étienne. Despite some success, including a trophy in the form of Ligue 1, the team's failure to win an European Cup was disappointing. Moreover, Platini's performances for the national team during this period were underwhelming, leading to France's failure to qualify for the 1980 Euros.

After his final season with Saint-Étienne, Platini took part in the 1984 World Cup in Spain. Despite a promising start, France suffered a heart-wrenching loss to Germany in the semifinals, a match that saw Platini score a goal. In the end, they fell short, even losing the third-place match to Poland.

Platini's career took a transformative turn when he joined Juventus. Partnering with Italian World Cup-winning players, he was expected to elevate the team to new heights. However, things didn't start smoothly, and Juventus faced a challenging period.

By winter, Juventus had gone seven matches without a win. But Platini refused to back down. He demanded a change in tactics that turned their fortunes around. Juventus only lost one more league match for the rest of the season and reached both the European Cup and the Coppa Italia finals.

The Coppa Italia final was particularly memorable. After a 2-0 defeat in the first leg, Platini scored a crucial goal in the second leg's dying moments, leading to extra time. He then scored another goal, sealing the trophy for Juventus in dramatic fashion.

Platini's brilliance continued in the following season. He scored 15 goals in 16 consecutive matches, leading Juventus to their first Serie A title in years. His outstanding performances earned him his first Ballon d'Or, highlighting his importance to the team's success.

But the pinnacle of his career came during the European Championships. Platini played a pivotal role, scoring consistently in every match he played. His seven goals in the tournament showcased his incredible talent. France ultimately won the Euros, with Platini being the star of the competition.

Platini's impact extended beyond the pitch. He held the record for the most consecutive matches scored in at the Euros and had the most goals scored in the final stages of the tournament, tied with Cristiano Ronaldo. His legacy was further enhanced by being the only player to achieve two hat-tricks in a single Euro tournament.

In the following season, Platini continued to shine. He helped Juventus win the Intercontinental Cup, adding to his growing list of trophies. His performance earned him his third consecutive Ballon d'Or, a remarkable achievement.

Unfortunately, tragedy struck during one of his greatest moments. The Heysel Stadium disaster, where fans were killed in a stadium collapse during a match, overshadowed Platini's European Cup victory with Juventus. Despite the triumph, it was a somber moment in his career.

The 1986 World Cup marked his last international tournament. Despite playing through injuries, he gave it his all. France reached the semifinals but suffered a heartbreaking loss to Germany in a match where Platini scored. They then lost the third-place match to Poland.

After his time with Juventus, Platini's career took a different path. He coached the French national team, achieving a record 19 consecutive wins. However, he stepped down after a disappointing early exit in the Euros.

Platini's journey had its ups and downs, but he left an indelible mark on the world of soccer. His legacy includes remarkable achievements and moments of brilliance, making him one of the greatest players in the history of the sport. His legacy is a mix of exceptional playmaking, dribbling, and an unrivaled icon factor. While he faced some adversity and had a shorter career, his impact on the game remains undeniable.

Do you know who the real superheroes of soccer are? It's not always the players who score goals; sometimes, it's the ones who stop them. These unsung heroes are the goalkeepers, and they don't often get the recognition they deserve.

Imagine your favorite soccer team playing without a goalkeeper. It would be chaos! Goalkeepers are like the last line of defense, the shield that protects the team's goal.

Now, some goalkeepers are just okay, but others are legendary. They make saves that seem impossible, and you can't help but wonder how they do it. One of those legendary goalkeepers was Lev Yashin. He's often called the greatest goalkeeper of all time.

Lev Yashin was born on October 22nd, 1929, in Moscow, Russia. But his journey to becoming a soccer legend was far from typical. When he was just 12 years old, World War II was raging, and instead of playing soccer like most kids his age, Yashin had to work in a factory to support the war effort. He spent six years doing hard labor.

At the age of 18, Yashin suffered a nervous breakdown, and his life took a different turn. He was transferred to a military factory in Moscow, where he found solace in playing soccer. The factory had its own soccer team, and Yashin joined it. Little did he know that this would be the beginning of an incredible soccer career.

Yashin's skills as a goalkeeper didn't go unnoticed. He was spotted by scouts from Dynamo Moscow, a top soccer club in the Soviet Union. Despite having to work in a factory, Yashin's talent couldn't be hidden, and he was invited to join the Dynamo Moscow youth team.

But here's something fascinating about Yashin – he wasn't just a soccer player. He was also an ice hockey player. He juggled both sports for the first four years of his soccer career. It wasn't until 1954 that he decided to focus solely on soccer.

Yashin's professional career began in 1950 when he made his debut for Dynamo Moscow. This was during a time when cameras didn't capture every moment of a player's career like they do today. So, we only have a fraction of the footage to appreciate his greatness.

During his 21-year career with Dynamo Moscow, Yashin achieved incredible success. He helped his team win five league titles and three cups. But his impact extended beyond the club level. Yashin played a pivotal role in the success of the Soviet national team. He led them to victory in the 1956 Summer Olympics and the 1960 European Championship. In the 1966 World Cup, he helped the team secure a fourth-place finish.

One of the most memorable moments of Yashin's career came in 1963 during a match between England and the Rest of the World. He made breathtaking saves that left spectators in awe and solidified his reputation as one of the greatest goalkeepers in history. That same year, Yashin achieved something unprecedented for a goalkeeper – he won the Ballon d'Or, an award typically reserved for outfield players.

But here's the sad part of Yashin's story. Despite his incredible talent and achievements, he remained relatively unknown to the rest of the world until the internet age. He played in the Soviet Union during a time of dictatorship, and few cameras captured his performances. It's only now, thanks to the internet, that we can appreciate his greatness fully.

So, next time you watch a soccer game, remember that the real superheroes might not be the ones scoring goals but the ones who save them. Lev Yashin, a legendary goalkeeper who defied the odds and became a true soccer icon.

Epilogue

Congratulations, young soccer enthusiast! You've reached the end of "Inspiring Soccer Stories for Young Readers: Mastering the Mental Toughness and Winning Mindset Strategies to Become an Amazing Soccer Player." As you close this book, you've not only learned about the history, rules, and strategies of the beautiful game but have also been inspired by the incredible journeys of both young soccer stars and legendary players.

Remember that soccer is more than just a sport; it's a canvas on which you can paint your dreams and aspirations. The lessons you've gleaned from these pages go beyond the field and can be applied to every aspect of your life. Here are a few final thoughts to carry with you on your continued soccer journey:

1. **Passion and Dedication:** Greatness in soccer, as in life, is often born from passion and dedication. Find your love for the game and nurture it. The more you practice and dedicate yourself to improving, the closer you'll get to your goals.

2. **Mental Toughness:** Soccer can be challenging but remember that your mindset plays a significant role in your success. Develop mental toughness by staying positive, setting goals, and persevering through setbacks. Embrace challenges as opportunities to grow.

3. **Teamwork:** Soccer is a team sport, and your success is closely linked to how well you work with your teammates. Learn to communicate effectively, support one another, and understand that victories are sweeter when shared.

4. **Never Stop Learning:** The world of soccer is constantly evolving. Keep learning, stay curious, and adapt to new techniques and strategies. Seek inspiration from the greats, and don't be afraid to develop your unique style.

5. **Dream Big:** As you've seen from the stories in this book, dreams can become reality with hard work and determination. Set ambitious goals, visualize your success, and chase your dreams with all your heart.

6. **Respect the Game:** Soccer is not just a sport; it's a global phenomenon that brings people together. Respect your

opponents, teammates, coaches, and referees. Sportsmanship and fair play are essential values on and off the field.

7. **Enjoy the Journey:** While winning is exhilarating, remember that the journey is just as important. Cherish the friendships you make, the lessons you learn, and the memories you create along the way.

As you step back onto the soccer pitch or continue your exploration of this beautiful game, know that the world of soccer is vast and full of opportunities. Whether you aspire to play for your school, local club, or even represent your country, the skills and mindset you've developed will serve as your compass.

Now, it's time to put this knowledge into practice, embrace the challenges, and, above all, enjoy the joy of playing soccer. Whether you're dribbling the ball, passing to a teammate, or taking a shot at goal, remember that you have the potential to be an amazing soccer player. Your journey is just beginning, and the future holds countless possibilities.

So, go ahead, chase your dreams, and write your own inspiring soccer story. The world of soccer eagerly awaits your unique contribution. Best of luck, young player, and may your soccer journey be filled with excitement, growth, and unforgettable moments on and off the field.

Made in the USA
Las Vegas, NV
18 December 2024

14610678R00095